Grants for Christian Ministries and *More!*

William F. High

Grants for Christian Ministries and More
by William F. High

Printed in the United States of America

ISBN 9781609572983

www.xulonpress.com

To
All the seekers who ask in faith and the givers who offer blessings
Matthew 7:7 and Acts 20:35

Contents

Introduction......*ix*
1. The Most Common Development Mistake......11
   - by Connie Hougland
2. The Perfect Storm—The Coming Charity Crisis......22
   - by William High
3. Researching Support Types and Funders......31
   - by Tom Ramirez
4. Building Biblical Relationships with Funders......39
   - by Bob Vickers
5. Legal and Governance Issues of Grant Seeking......43
   - By Michelle Adams
6. A Perspective from the Grant Maker and Grant Writer......54
   - by Gene Rietfors
7. The Professional Grant Writer......63
   - by Joyce Leggette
8. Writing the Grant Proposal......70
   - by Gil Mertz
9. Presenting a Compelling Statement of Need......79
   - by Ben Evans
10. Drafting the Budget......88
    - by Maricia Johns
11. Approaching Secular Funders......93
    - by Joy Skjegstad

12. Applying for Federal Faith-Based Grants 104
- by Hal Merz
13. Writing the Federal Faith-Based Grant Proposal 114
- by Cheryl Kester
14. Planned Giving Success for Small Nonprofits 124
- by Bob Crew
15. Creative Alternatives to Foundation Giving 135
- by Debbie Farrar
16. Starting a Church Foundation 142
-by William High
Glossary 155
Notes 165

Introduction

So why this book? I don't think there is a need for yet another book on fundraising. But this book is not about fundraising. It's about how your ministry or church can receive grants *and more*. To accomplish that end, we've put together a collaborative work: we obtained some of the best at their craft and had them contribute a chapter. The idea behind this collaboration is that you will receive different views on various topics; it's not just one author and his ideas on the subject.

This book contains chapters on the grant process, writing a grant, preparing the budget, and two chapters on federal grant writing. But we don't stop there—hence the name *Grants for Christian Ministries And More!* The "and more" includes—*The Perfect Storm—The Coming Charity Crisis*. This chapter presents some of the demographic issues that call for charities to adjust like never before. Then, the "and more" continues into chapters like "planned giving" and "alternatives to foundation giving." All of the chapters are designed to help your ministry advance to the next level in your funding.

As for the grant writing section of the book, why is it so important to learn how to write a grant? Can't anyone just "make it up as he or she goes along?" Well, there are 1.5 million nonprofits in the United States, but only about 110,000 private grant-making foundations.[1] And of those private foundations, less than half accept applications for grants.[2] In order to effectively compete for grants, your organization must understand how to write compelling, concise proposals that neatly answer the grant maker's questions.

Now, what is a grant proposal? Simply defined, a grant proposal is a written request for support. It seems like it ought to be a simple process. Yet, even the very thought of grant writing strikes fear into the hearts of many nonprofit employees. There is something that just does not sound appealing about haphazardly crunching through mounds of data searching for potential funders, blending numbers together until the blotchy muddle looks vaguely like a multi-year budget, or messily plowing through descriptive synonyms as you attempt to write a perfect proposal with sensational success stories, inspirational ideas, and brilliant budgets. Okay. Stop for a moment now and breathe. All is not lost. If you follow the tips in this book and review each section of the grant application and follow its instructions, the task will not seem so insurmountable.

Supporting your ministry is an ongoing work. Or perhaps more aptly, an ongoing learning process. Learn all that you can because in the learning you develop a greater understanding and appreciation for God the Father, our ultimate provider.

May God bless you as you begin your grant writing journey!

William F. High

Chapter 1

The Most Common Development Mistake

By Connie Hougland

As a representative of a Christian community foundation, I've had the joy of listening to hundreds of ministries tell their stories of how God impacts the world through their work. One day, as I sat listening to a well-established, respected ministry talk about its development plan, it happened again. The dreaded statement and request, "All I need is the name of one rich Christian with deep pockets." That's when the nagging question first surfaced: how is it that so many well-intentioned, God-seeking ministries miss the boat when it comes to serving donors?

The big idea is that development is not about us. It is not strictly a role. It is not a checklist. And, it is not just a means to an end. Rather, development is itself a ministry, a way of life. And yet, too many of us paint targets on the backs of wealthy Christians and funders and approach development in a dry, passionless way.

If I were to ask you why you are in ministry – why you do what you do – I would likely be captivated by your passion. I would also guess that without any prompting you would share with me about the people you serve. You would tell me about their needs, their challenges and your desire for them to see God's perfect design for them. You have a vision for them.

Typically there is no lack of passion within the ministry community. We have passion for the cause, passion for the people, passion for the call, passion for the Kingdom. . . .

However, if I were to ask you about your development plan for your ministry would I hear the same passion? Is a development plan and those who give merely a means to the end? Are givers (individuals and foundations) just a necessary evil needed to complete your mission? All we really need is for someone with deep pockets to catch the fever and fund the whole thing, right?

Even if we don't consciously see our givers as a necessary evil I wonder if our message and actions inadvertently portray it that way. What would it look like if development became a ministry, a way of life?

Development is a Ministry

We know that God's greatest resource is people. So, it would make sense that God's economy would include utilizing His greatest resource to support and fund ministry. Our development plan is not only a means to an end but a vital ministry to *people*.

I would argue that there are two sides to the "coin" of a development plan. First, and most obvious, there is the side of the ministry. As a ministry we are meeting and addressing the needs of the people we serve. Equally important, however, is the side of the giver – the steward. Development as a ministry addresses both aspects.

A Closer Look at the Two-Sided Coin

Here we are a great ministry – a valid ministry – a needed ministry – we are filling a gap – we sacrifice for others – we are serving – we are advancing God's Kingdom – we are relevant – we are good stewards – we are Called – let's face it we rock. The reality is that all we need is more money. If people only knew the sacrifices we've made, how hard we have worked – they would realize how deserving we are. We need their money to keep going. We dream of that rich donor, Mr. Deep Pockets; if he could just write that big check, the problem would be solved.

Take a moment to put yourself in the shoes of Mr. Deep Pockets. He is a successful business owner, sacrificing family for the sake of business, he desires to be a good steward and he desires to be relevant in advancing God's Kingdom. Everyone wants a piece of him. He is loved for his money, and he receives hundreds of desperate requests for help. He wonders who cares about him and who just cares about his money.

The reality is our givers are on a journey – a giving journey. Givers have their own questions: Why have I been given so much? How would God expect me to steward this? Where should it be deployed? Givers want to be a part of something bigger than themselves. They want to be part of a winning team. They want to fund a cause not a sinking ship. These are God's givers not OUR donors.

Remember earlier we talked about the misnomer that "all we need is a wealthy Christian"? The logic of this statement is that money is the answer. It would seem that if money were the answer the problem would have been solved a long time ago. There is a lot of money floating around this world. Money isn't the answer. God's people responding in their heart to God's call to give is the answer. It's a heart issue not a dollar symbol issue. It's time we put a face to the dollar sign.

We must be open to a paradigm shift to be about serving givers not targeting them. It is about nurturing long-term relationships not just receiving a check. Our part is to be faithful; it is God who gives the increase. We cannot control how much is given, but we can control how we involve and engage people. In development we do not raise money; rather, we advance mission. We engage people in meaningful involvement in the life of the ministry.

One way to tackle the giver side of the coin is to think about your own giving. How do you make your decisions to give? Are your giving decisions reactionary or strategic? How do you choose whom you give to? Do you give to desperation or big vision? How did you learn about the organizations you give to? When you learn about a new ministry what is the first question you ask? What are your preferred methods for giving?

It would be a worthwhile exercise to walk through similar questions with your team to see how your answers to your personal giving compare to the activities that make up your ministry's development plan. Ask the question, how can we engage in a paradigm shift to be about serving donors vs. targeting donors? How can our development plan balance the needs of our ministry with the needs of our givers?

Advancing Mission

If development is not raising money but advancing mission then we need to take one more step back. A good development plan begins with an honest evaluation of our ministry. From a holistic perspective, how does our ministry fit within the whole plan – God's plan? Do we recognize that we are just a part of the plan? We are not THE answer. Advancing mission is not just understanding the call and purpose of our ministry but how it fits into God's plan.

It is important to understand your unique niche. Figure out what you do best and stick to it. Much like the calling of the Body of Christ – we each play a specific role but put together we are a complete reflection of Christ. As you know more about what God is doing through other ministries you can better appreciate your specific part. Get to know other ministries. Be intentional about looking for connecting and collaboration opportunities. Remember, donors (and certainly foundations) typically give to more than one ministry. There are few things more invigorating to givers and funders than seeing organizations work together. Think about providing givers with the opportunity to be a part of something bigger than they could have imagined.

Don't Just Walk the Walk. Talk the Walk.

A review of your development plan means taking a close look at your messaging and communications. What you say about what you do is as important as how well you do what you do.

Earlier I said that passion is important in conveying your vision but sometimes we can become so caught up in our passion for the call of our ministry that we overwhelm those we invite to join us in the journey. Remember givers have passion too. You want to connect with those passions from the perspective of the giver, not from a soapbox. The expertise found throughout this book will give you great counsel on how to clearly communicate your message to potential funders. Keep these ideas in mind as you communicate to individual donors as well. Give them the opportunity to ask the next question. Give them enough clear but compelling information that they want to know more about how they can be a part of what God is doing through your ministry. Speak their language – talk to them, not at them. Give them a clear understanding that they can be a part of something bigger than themselves. Show them how your ministry is part of and fits into God's plan.

Our ability to articulate our mission and vision in a compelling way is key to reaching and maintaining givers. We all want to be part of a winning team. While the needs you are addressing are big and yes, even overwhelming, the reality is that there will never be a shortfall of needs. Givers like to know what IS working. What kind of impact are you having? How are lives being transformed? We don't want to dismiss the beauty of what it means when one life is changed. As we think about Jesus' ministry, He served the masses. . . .individually. With Jesus it is always personal. He was thinking of me (you) when He breathed His last breath. He did it for us all – but it was personal. Likewise, you will want to use personal stories of how God reaches people through your ministry. Show givers what success looks like for actual people.

Messaging designed around our givers is directed to them and is about them. It understands what they are going through as givers. Also remember, speak the language of your givers and talk to them, not at them. Although you know what MUPG means, you cannot assume your giver understands this refers to Muslim unreached people groups. When you must use technical terms like this, make their meanings clear through context. Finally, keep in mind that personal does not mean unprofessional. Professionalism is a must. God's givers deserve our very best. Spend the time to proofread. If your ministry can be trusted with the little things like spelling, grammar, and basic marketing, you are much more likely to be trusted with the important matter of stewarding giving dollars.

To recap, in order to make development a ministry, a way of life, our plan needs to be about how we engage and serve our donors. One of my favorite book titles on fundraising is *Donors are People Too* (I will take it a step further and say "Foundations are People Too"). We need that reminder, don't we?

If we think about our ministry to givers (people) what is it they need?

- They need a compelling vision (people will give more to a compelling vision than a compelling need)
- They need to know they are a part of something
- They need to understand the impact
- They need an easy way to give
- They need a way to give that meets their needs

The How of Giving

The more tactical side of building your development plan should be donor-focused as well. Your funding plan must be diverse and broad-reaching.

Traditionally development plans consist of:

- Individual giving – monthly donors
- Church giving
- Direct mail / Annual appeals
- Campaigns
- Annual event / Special events
- Planned Giving
- Foundations / Grants

These are all great tactics and things we should continue. But we live in a time that we need to look beyond the traditional if we desire growth.

Cutting edge development plans also include:

- Earned-Income / Revenue Sources
- Online and Noncash Giving
- Major Donor Services – Asset Giving

By looking at earned-income ventures it may be possible for a ministry to generate new and unrestricted revenue and decrease reliance on traditional fundraising activities. At the same time, earned-income ventures will require time, money and concentrated effort to make them succeed. Look for natural markets to begin your venture. What is it that fits best with what you know and what you currently do as a ministry? Coffee shops are obvious choices for churches. Maybe your organization assists with job training for orphans in Africa. Can you find a way to help them sell their wares in the United States?

As with any new journey you will need to work through the issues that help to evaluate the cost versus the benefits of branching out in this area. Numerous resources are available online regarding this new trend, often called "social entrepreneurship."

Expanding the *how* people can give to your ministry may represent the biggest opportunity yet. Having a broad base of ways donors can engage emphasizes the idea that your development plan is about them, not you.

Many of us have expanded the way givers can give cash or liquid gifts through online giving (credit/debit card, eChecks), automatic giving (ACH), and publicly traded stock giving. These giving strategies are a ***must,*** but let's look beyond the checkbook.

Statistically, giving is done in the form of cash, but the world's wealth is in noncash assets. Some 80%-85% of giving is cash-based, but 91% of the wealth of the world is in the things we own – our cars, boats, RVs, real estate, businesses and more. As ministries we target the checkbook. We capture the heartstrings of the donor and then tell them to look at the most limited resource in their portfolio to engage with us. Unintentionally, we are encouraging a scarcity mentality with givers. We are asking them to think limited when it comes to giving. Think about it for a minute. If cash represents only 9% of the wealth but 80% of how giving is done, we are missing a huge opportunity to *serve* givers!

Along these same lines, you can better serve major donors with asset giving. Remember Mr. Deep Pockets? He was juggling his family, his business, and his desire to be a good steward. By introducing asset giving, your ministry has an opportunity to truly serve Mr. Deep Pockets.

Let's look at what an asset gift might mean to Mr. Deep Pockets. Let's assume his business is worth $10 million and has an annual income of $1 million. He caps his lifestyle at $200,000, gives $30,000 in cash giving and has a $400,000 tax bill. By opening the door to noncash giving Mr. Deep Pockets could give a 3% interest in his business (nonvoting shares) to charity. The net result would increase his giving amount to $330,000 and decrease his tax bill to $280,000. Talk about serving donors. By serving Mr. Deep Pockets versus targeting him we just increased his giving capacity one hundred fold.

The above example is notably complex. The good news is that ministries do not have to tackle this alone. There are Christian organizations committed to providing this type of service to ministries. You don't have to figure it out on your own. The goal is to increase the serve to givers without diverting the ministry from its mission. As a practical step, learn more about the Christian community foundation movement at www.nationalchristian.com. Their local network provides partnership opportunities for ministries to have the abilities and expertise necessary to serve givers in this area. An additional resource for smaller noncash giving is www.idonate.com.

As we serve more and target less we get to be part of creating giving evangelists. There is no greater marketing tool for your ministry than a donor who is using his/her influence to cast a giving vision for other donors.

Yea, God!

It might seem odd at first, but your development plan should also include celebration. The power of celebration is many-fold. It can serve as a renewal and re-energizer for your team. It means we are stopping and saying, "Yes, Lord, we acknowledge how you are working through us. And, we give You the Glory." It means that we are validating our givers, volunteers and workers. It can give us strength to continue and remind us this work is worth it. Do not underestimate the power of celebration.

While there are no magic formulas when it comes to development planning, consider looking for ways to design your plan around givers. Take inventory and consider where you are. Do you believe the need for resources outpaces the capacity of givers? Or, do you believe that God is the God who owns the cattle on a thousand hills – that His resources are plentiful and wide? If we develop our plan with a scarcity mentality then scarcity is what we will get. If you take only one thing away from this chapter, then it should be that giving is about the need of the giver not strictly the needs of the ministry. Giving is a God-given gift to be part of something bigger than yourself. It is an action of the heart, and a measure of the heart. Let's not miss the opportunity to minister to the hearts of givers. That should be the driving force and passion behind our development ministry for givers to experience the true joy and fullness of life that comes from giving with all their hearts. Be encouraged – God is at work! May He bless you as you serve in His name.

~~~

Connie Hougland is a Vice President with the Servant Christian Community Foundation (www.servantchristian.com). She may be reached at chougland@servantchristian.com. Servant's mission is to inspire, teach and facilitate revolutionary biblical generosity. Servant works with givers, ministries and financial advisors to help increase giving using cash and noncash assets.
~~~

Chapter 2

The Perfect Storm—the Coming Charity Crisis

By William High

Summary of Article:

Few people in the church and ministry world have adequately recognized how the coming demographics will shape the landscape of our world. In the United States, the population base is growing older while the birth rate is flat. This means that fewer people will support more people. They will do so with less income, greater tax burden, and less charitable deduction opportunity. On the other hand, the ministry world has an unprecedented opportunity to capture wealth, including noncash assets, that will influence the spread of the Gospel.

Introduction

The Perfect Storm. It's a term used to describe when all the necessary conditions collide for disastrous purposes. In the next thirty years, perfect storm conditions exist for charities around the world. This article will address what those conditions are, and what charities must do to address those conditions.

Demographic Issues

The world's population is nearing 7 billion people. China represents the largest number of people with 1.3 billion people. The United States represents a small fraction of the world's population with just 300 million people. Birth rates continue to climb in China, India and Africa. Meanwhile, birth rates in Europe are declining, and largely flat in the United States.

What are the implications from these birth rates? Without a continued influx of youth, Europe will rely largely on immigration for its workers. The United States will realize an increasing dependency on foreign labor. For instance, by the year 2030, it's predicted that the United States will have a 29% decline in doctors and a shortage of at least 1 million nurses. Where will those doctors and nurses come from? They will come from those countries producing people: India, China, Africa.

On the other hand, the birth rates have an equally important implication on the other end of the spectrum. The world's population is getting older, particularly the United States population.

Advances in medical technology mean that people can live longer. New research, new cures, new medicines give people increased opportunity to live longer. By 2030, 19% of the United States population will be age 65 and older.

Of course, with an older population base, there are a number of implications:

1. Some will require more care.
2. There will be a greater burden upon the health care system.

3. While some of these elderly people will be productive workers, many will not be. And in any event, these people generally will not be at their peak earning years.
4. These people will not bear the tax burden for the country.

These implications do not even begin to address the issues of unfunded entitlement programs. Imagine nearly 20% of the United States population receiving Social Security and receiving Medicare or Medicaid benefits. Where will those dollars come from?

For the young people of our country, the picture remains equally gloomy. They will carry the nation's tax burden. They will be called upon to support more and more people requiring more care. And they will do so with less income. Generally, education rates are declining among our youth. In short, our children of today will be less prosperous than previous generations. To meet the crushing social service needs of our country, they will likely face the highest income tax burden any generation has ever faced.

The Brave New World of Charity

These demographic and financial issues have far-reaching impact on ministries and churches. It is doubtful that few churches and ministries even realize the coming wave of opportunity and challenge. Some will not survive. They will shut their doors. Let's examine why.

The number of people needing services will increase. Think about it. Today, the most efficient and effective social service delivery system rests within the nonprofit world—not government. With nearly 20% of the population being age 65 and older, there will be more people requiring more care.

The government will be stretched to provide those services. The government's limits will be tested by a variety of factors. Social Security, Medicare and Medicaid remain a critical part of the care of the elderly in our country. But they are unfunded. There is no trust fund, as it was originally designed, supporting these payments. These payments will have to come from a younger population base that is not growing. In other words, fewer people will be supporting more people.

On the other hand, as the government is stretched to provide those services, it will be looking for revenue. The first place it will have to look will be tax increases. Thus, those same people who are supporting more people will likely do so with a much higher tax burden.

Higher tax burdens mean less disposable income. Less disposable income means lower giving. And keep in mind that as the government looks for revenue, one of the places it will look will be in reducing, or dare we say it, eliminating the charitable deduction. The charitable deduction represents 300 billion dollars of potential tax revenue for a cash-hungry government.

Already there has been some erosion in the charitable deduction. The vehicle deduction was severely curtailed. Proposals have been on the table to eliminate property tax exemptions for nonprofit hospitals. Elimination of fair market value deductions for real estate has been on the table in the Senate. More proposals will most assuredly be coming.

Consider the plight then of the upcoming generation. They'll face the challenge of supporting more people, with higher taxes, less money in their pocket, and perhaps even little or no deduction for their giving.

These conditions will test the purity of an individual's giving. But it will also test the strength of the church or nonprofit's mission. Those who cast a compelling vision and serve the needs of their people will survive.

Moreover, the church and nonprofit must do a better job of educating their givers. Giving is not a mechanical percentage-setting act; it is an outflow of the heart. Giving which is driven by arm-twisting capital campaigns, agenda or ego-driven needs will not work in a cash-strapped world. Teaching people to give generously and sacrificially for their own spiritual growth is key. This education issue alone may well determine who survives and who falls.

How Churches and Nonprofits Should Respond

As the ministry world looks forward, there is significant opportunity to prepare. We can capture the opportunity through education of givers, major donor cultivation and pursuit of noncash donations, growth of enterprise-based funding and development of endowment funding.

Education of Givers

Education of givers must be pursued at every level. Programs like Crown Financial Ministries, Good Sense, and Dave Ramsey must be employed. These programs all vary somewhat but cover the basic principles:

1. God owns it all.
2. Man is a steward/manager.
3. Part of being a steward is staying out of debt.
4. Giving is not based upon percentages but upon how much God has blessed us.
5. We are accountable for our use of God's resources.

By pursuing the education of givers, we create a common language and a common culture of generosity. That is the key: developing a culture of generous people. Generous people are by nature happy people for the simple reason that they reflect the character of Christ.

Those people who reflect this generous nature will be people who will give no matter what the circumstances are—tax deduction or not. These people will also not impose artificial limits on giving; they may be people who will give 90% of their income.

Major Donor Cultivation

While education involves the masses, major donor cultivation focuses upon those individuals with the greatest capacity to make a difference with a single gift. The adage is true in any church or ministry: 20% of the people tend to support 80% of the budget. That fact alone supports the necessity of major donor cultivation.

Major donor cultivation is particularly important in unstable economies. In every economy, there will inevitably be those businesses that will be hitting home runs. Those people have been blessed with a unique opportunity to give and advance a ministry. A major donor means those who have the ability to make a contribution of $100,000 or more. It's important to recognize that there are those with the ability to make contributions even above $1 million.

Major donor cultivation starts with the recognition that the needs of the major donor are different. Major donors need safety and relationship—the ability to share their issues without fear that someone is going to ask them for money. The complexity of their situation is different, and not just from a financial perspective. They have huge questions surrounding them: who will succeed them in business? Will they ruin their children if they leave them too much? How do they reward key employees? Are there relationships that need restoration?

The major donor needs to build a community of like minded people around him or her. The Gathering and Generous Giving provide two venues for the best safety and community.

Pursuit of Noncash Donations

Most donations (80% or more) are done in the form of cash. On the other hand, the vast majority of wealth, 90%, resides in noncash assets. Noncash assets are things like cars, boats, RVs, collectibles, real estate, and business interests. Stated differently, when people think about giving, few think about giving noncash assets.

It remains untapped but therefore a significant opportunity for giving. To illustrate, we worked with an individual whose company was doing extremely well. They could give significant cash gifts that amounted to a few hundred thousand dollars. But when he realized he could give some of the stock of his closely held company, he elevated his giving to the $1 million range.

We've now seen people make value choices in their giving. They give things like a car, a boat, or an RV because they know the asset can be sold and the proceeds given to the Kingdom. As people realize they can give assets, they get creative about their giving and reach into their financial statement for things like stamp collections, jewelry and even business-inventory gifts.

In the coming years, asset-based gifts represent a huge multi-billion dollar opportunity. One asset-based provider is www.idonate.com.

Enterprise Funding

As people pursue creative gifting, an interesting trend is developing: 47% of nonprofits are developing business ventures to fund their work. This may be as simple as creating a coffee shop that brings in a bit of revenue to a full blown product line of sportswear that provides a bigger chunk of the budget.

This enterprise-funding model provides a unique way to get people involved in the work but also a way to involve the business owner. Business owners know how to build businesses and create revenue. They can use those same talents to build a business where the "profit" would go to the church or ministry.

For example, three businessmen combined to purchase a prime piece of development ground. They helped lead the efforts to locate a Christian school on that ground. They are now selling off outparcels to retail businesses. The profits from the outparcel are going directly to the school. Additionally, they are now working on a plan where one of those retail businesses will be owned by the charity, and the profits from the business will go directly into the business. A side bonus is that many of the workers for the business can come from the Christian school.

This enterprise funding, coupled with the noncash innovations, represent by far one of the great untapped energies available to ministry in the coming years.

Development of Endowment Funding

Notwithstanding the current economic conditions, we are in the midst of the greatest wealth transfer in the history of the world. The Depression Era generation is almost gone. The World War II generation is similarly in their waning years. The Boomers are turning 60. Within these three generations is the greatest repository of wealth the world has ever known.

One fact is clear: they will all die, and they will all transfer their wealth. There is a limited amount of time behind this wealth transfer - 20 to 30 years at most. This wealth transfer has been estimated to be $40 trillion. The use of foundations and endowments becomes more critical. A foundation or endowment maintains principal but works off from the income generated by the principal.

The instruction for the church and nonprofit world is to capture this wealth transfer. Indeed, in Genesis, Joseph used the seven years of prosperity to store up wealth for the coming lean years. Joseph's example should be heeded by the ministry world today.

Because we know this wealth transfer is occurring, we need to act quickly and decisively to capture it. Notably, much of this wealth transfer is in noncash assets. Likewise, in heeding the example of Joseph, the temptation to spend all the wealth transfer once it is captured must be avoided. Instead, some of that wealth must be stored for the lean times ahead.

A Final Word

Not all is gloomy, however. As the church looks globally and thinks about completing the Great Commission, it's difficult to fully predict all the implications. There is little doubt that the world population centers of China, India, and Africa will require real and significant attention. While some of the economic conditions may seem dismal, the coming days promise to be some of the most exciting in the history of the world.

The work of the Gospel will advance worldwide. People will be motivated by the knowledge that we can get the job done, and they will respond accordingly. I believe the saints who have gone before us will pull those of us in this generation aside and inquire about what it was like to live in the days where the Gospel was advancing so forcefully.

~~~

William F. High is the President/General Counsel of the Servant Christian Community Foundation (www.servantchristian.com). He may be reached at whigh@servantchristian.com. Servant's mission is to inspire, teach and facilitate revolutionary biblical generosity. Servant works with givers, ministries and financial advisors to help increase giving using cash and noncash assets.
~~~

Chapter 3

Researching Support Types and Funders

By Tom Ramirez

I recently attended a summit for nonprofit representatives and program officers of private foundations. Their discussions betrayed the nonprofit sector's lack of identity. I heard many organizations describe funding needs with a pervasive sense of victimization as they asked for a financial rescuer. In one small group comprised primarily of social service agencies, I challenged the ministries to see their value from a marketing perspective, especially in cause-related marketing partnerships with businesses that wish to demonstrate their company's social consciousness by supporting a cause. Understanding your ministry's value will set you apart from those who take a "beggar's posture." Once you recognize your ministry's value, you are ready to begin the search for grants.

Writing grant proposals can be a daunting and frustrating experience initially; but like everything else, the process becomes easier with experience. In this chapter, we will discuss the various types of support and how to research funders. Often, the most difficult part of the proposal is getting started, which is why we will discuss as many practical steps as possible. However, the process is more of an art than an exact science.

Types of Support

To begin the grant process, review your ministry and its programs to determine the support types you need. Then, research foundation giving trends and the types of support foundations emphasize. Below are several examples of support types:

- Operating support involves general support or unrestricted income that covers the cost of running an organization.
- Special projects usually occur within a restricted time frame, such as starting a new program or expanding one.
- Capacity building enables a nonprofit to increase its fundraising or administrative capacity to support program growth.
- Capital or equipment (brick and mortar) funds provide for new or expansion construction, remodeling, renovation, land acquisition, or equipment needed for the ministry's physical buildings.
- Endowments are usually obtained through planned giving where the principal is held as a long-term investment for the organization. Then, this income is used for operating needs.

Researching Funders

The second step of the grant proposal process involves researching funders. A foundation rarely provides all of the funding for a given project, and certainly not all of the support necessary for operating expenses or building campaigns. Foundations also expect organizations to invest their own in-kind resources in the project and to obtain funding from diverse sources. Diversifying funding verifies your credibility and your organization's capacity to maintain long-term sustainability.

Researching funders begins by understanding three primary grant sources:

- Government agencies - federal, state, and local city or county. Accessing these funds usually begins with a Request for Proposal (RFP) from a government agency such as the Department of Justice, Department of Education, Department of Health and Human Services, etc. These funds are sometimes more speculative than private funds because they offer demonstration grants to explore new approaches for identified problems. For example, the government may fund faith-based programs addressing alcohol and substance abuse, or programs for the chronically homeless. Government funds are a good starting place because they may offer significant support for your project. Also, many private funders may ask if you have exhausted government grant opportunities before approaching them.
- Private Foundations - A nongovernmental, nonprofit organization with funds (usually established by a single source, such as an individual, family, or corporation) and initiatives managed by its own trustees or directors. A private operating foundation is a private foundation or charitable trust that spends at least 85 percent of its adjusted net income or its minimum investment return, whichever is less, directly for exempt activities. There are more than 110,000 pri-

vate foundations in the United States, and more than half of them have assets less than $1 million.

- Corporate Foundations - created by a for-profit company to support its community or activities that complement the goals of the business. The company's foundation may be a separate entity funded through ongoing contributions or endowments as opposed to the company's optional benevolence fund used for smaller donations.

Researching funders usually requires access to a subscription-based database. Subscriptions to these proprietary databases vary from $90 - $500 annually; they may also provide limited access on a monthly or daily basis. Finally, local libraries may offer free access to funder databases on an appointment basis.

With so many funders, how do you find the right one? I suggest the following steps:

Step 1: Focus your search. Look for federal or state funding that suits your project. Be aware of application deadlines and allow plenty of time for the complexities accompanying these funding sources.

Next, research private and corporate foundations. Subscribe to newsletters that provide information, training, or grant writing services. Some of these newsletters will notify you of upcoming grant proposal deadlines. Search subscription-based services with various query fields: purpose and activities of the foundation, areas of interest, types of support, geographic focus, and limitations.

Step 2: After your initial search, prioritize prospective funders by finding additional detailed information. Look at the funder's website, or write to the foundation and request an information packet. Once you receive the packet, look for these items:

- A list of trustees; see if there are any connections with your board of directors.
- Application deadlines; dates trustees meet.
- Instructions for Letters of Inquiry and applications.
- Size of grants.
- Emphasis on certain geographic areas.
- Grant details or program notes for clarification of types of programs funded or first-time grant request limitations.
- Eligibility requirements.
- Amount of total giving in last reported year.
- Range of grant amounts awarded.
- Distribution percentages to areas of emphasis.
- Other pertinent information to determine whether you should pursue funding from this foundation.

Step 3: Request a copy of the funder's last annual report or look for it on its website. Many times an IRS Form 990 or 990 PDF is available to download from the funder's website or from a nonprofit reporting agency. Once you receive this report, look closely at the program areas and the types of organizations the funder supports. When the grant is from federal or state sources, find the original legislation that established the purpose and guidelines for the program's funding.

Step 4: Prepare to contact the funder. It is important to build good relationships with funders, because they do not want to be seen as vending machines. Compile a list of questions you want to ask the grant administrator or program officer. Here are some examples:

- "Please clarify your funding priorities and the types of funding you award." In lieu of asking them to review their published criteria, ask them to clarify your understanding of their foundation.
- "What criteria do you use to grade proposals - e.g. community need, confidence in organization to deliver outcomes?" (Many times funders have a template of criteria they use to grade organizations when meeting with them.)
- "What nuances might be overlooked by just reading the published guidelines that identify your values and areas of interest?"
- "What 'exchange' do you want for your gift?" (usually a type of recognition) "What is valuable to you and your foundation?"

Also, prepare to answer questions *they* ask to determine if you are a good fit for them.

- Create a brief description of your project or ministry.
- Describe what events transpired that made your ministry aware of a need or inspired your organization's call to ministry
- Prepare an answer as to *why* you are doing your ministry. Have short success stories ready that convey your passion for your mission.

Step 5: Contact the prospective funder. Plan for a 10 to 15 minute telephone interview. The conversation should not be a blatant sales pitch, but a relaxed conversation where you exchange information. Remember, you are building a relationship, not applying for a loan.

You can try to schedule a meeting with the grants administrator or program officer, but chances of a face-to-face meeting become less likely as you draw nearer to the application deadline. It is often easier to communicate with a busy program officer by email rather than telephone or an in-person meeting. This type of communication will force both of you to be more succinct as well.

Whatever type of contact you make, assure the funder that you have "reviewed their application guidelines and foundation reports and that you have just a few specific questions to determine how closely your project aligns with their objectives." Again, they are not just a source of funds for your ministry; they want to make a difference in the world with the resources at their disposal (in-kind, financial, volunteers), so they are looking for an "on-the-ground" partner to implement their objectives.

Finally, if you wait to contact the funder until the last weeks before the deadline, you convey a lack of good planning—a poor message you do not want to send to a foundation that is evaluating your ability to manage your project/program.

<u>Step 6:</u> Complete your final targeted list of prospective grant makers. Eliminate those who do not fit. Do not stretch your program focus to accommodate a funder's area of interest. Chasing funder dollars will only compromise your program, stress your staff with new requirements, and prevent your organization from accomplishing your outcome promises. You can always approach a funder later with another project that better fits its objectives. After all, a funder's objectives or areas of interest, as well as your needs, may change with time.

A Values-based approach

Finally, although most organizations seek funding by presenting a problem, values-based organizations frequently concentrate on adding value to a community. Examples of values-based organizations include cultural centers, performing arts programs, museums, religious activities, and libraries. The key to obtaining funding is to find funders with the same values as your organization.

~~~

Tom Ramirez is a professional grant writer with over seven years experience of writing for Christian organizations that assist missions projects, benevolence services, human services, and health care agencies. He has achieved funding success by developing a comprehensive Proposal Development Process. The components of the Proposal Development Process include these steps: developing a clear program plan that helps compile a Funder Preparedness Packet, thorough research of potential funders, building strong relationships with funders, targeting proposals carefully, and writing a concise proposal.
~~~

Chapter 4

Building Biblical Relationships with Funders

By Bob Vickers

After almost three decades of helping faith-based and community leaders access funding and other resources, I have learned to counsel people with the same biblical principles because the Bible doesn't change. Although I don't use religious words, the principles are rooted in Scripture and work because the Bible works.

One of the most important steps in the grant proposal process involves building relationships with funders. Because there are thousands of nonprofits in the United States alone, it is very difficult to obtain grants without a previous relationship with the funder. There are over 1.5 million IRS-recognized nonprofits in the U.S., and this number does not include churches.[3] Guess how many of these organizations need money? All of them!

There is a three-step process involved in building relationships with funders. However, let's first define biblical relationships.

"Building Biblical Relationships with Funders. . ."

What is meant by "building?" Relationships cannot function without communication. Communication is hard work, but most people commit to implementing it in marriage, parenting, jobs, and friendships, so it should not be neglected in funding relationships.

Realize that "building" is the entire farming process, not just harvesting a crop. See beyond your immediate need for cash to understand the population you serve, the people who serve alongside you, and those who support you.

What is meant by "biblical?" As a Christian, you must look at philanthropy differently and seek to understand the responsibility entrusted to you. First, *be* (personally develop) and then *do* (love your neighbor as yourself). Compare your grant writing and fundraising methods to Scriptural models and concepts. You cannot violate biblical principles and expect to be successful.

What is meant by "relationships?" As seen in Scripture, there are many qualities necessary for successful relationships. Before you approach potential donors, learn who they are and what interests them even if you do not directly see a connection with them. Remember to treat donors with respect, honor, dignity, and affirmation.

What is meant by "with funders?" While you need to know which foundations, community foundations, corporations, individuals, state, and federal funding sources are available, do not forget the supporters already around you—board members, family, community, and other churches. While donations may refer to money, giving also includes time, energy, expertise, relationships, connections, encouragement, vision, support, affirmation, inspiration, and much more.

Now that the definition of biblical relationships has been explored, we will discuss the three basic steps in building relationships with funders.

Building Relationships through Grant Writing

- Share Vision. Your grant proposal should reflect your vision in a compelling and concise manner as you describe how your ministry meets needs. The effectiveness of your proposal is two-thirds content and one-third format. What you say and how you say it matters.
- Research. Once you have created a list of potential funders, begin researching them at your local library or on any of the online funder databases. Read each funder's IRS 990 form and note the areas of interest, geographic focus, contact information, and other details important for relationship building.
- Be a good steward of your relationships—you probably have more contacts with funders than you realize. Wisely manage your relationships with volunteers, board members, corporations, and foundations in your city, state, and region.
- Engage. The third step involves building relationships in everything from rejection, approval, large gift or widow's mite. Ten lepers acquired what they wanted from Jesus, but only one returned to thank Him – and all had received what they wanted![4] Even if you don't feel appreciative, ask God to change your heart and allow you to express sincere gratitude.
- Write an immediate thank you note when you receive a grant or other support. Appreciate the $100,000 dollar gift and the $50 dollar gift. When you are rejected, be gracious and thank the funder for his or

her time and for meeting the needs of people in your community.

Final Challenge

While all the little details in grant proposal writing may seem overwhelming, don't overanalyze—just go for it. Visit a sporting goods store and buy a pair of knee pads. Take a permanent marker and write on them, "I can't. But He can! Philippians 4:13 and Philippians 4:19." Then, put them to work and stay on your knees. Seek God daily even if it means rug burns on your forehead. Buy a pair of knee pads for each member of your staff and board of directors and challenge them to join you in asking for God's provision.

Remember, there is no human need that lacks divine provision. God is doing a tremendous work in the world through faithful, humble, and obedient servants who take the time to learn, engage, and then teach others to build biblical relationships. God wants our hearts, our yielded spirits, and our desire to love Him and to serve His way. Are you willing to do that?

~~~

Bob Vickers is the founder and president of Artful Askers, a consulting workshop that has taught more than 24,000 nonprofits and churches how to access funding. His materials and life's work emphasize building biblical characteristics into various relationships: dating, marriage, family, friendships, church, community, and funding. Bob has written for many organizations including numerous international missions organizations. Currently, he is completing his doctorate in philosophy at Oxford Graduate School.
~~~

Chapter 5

Legal and Governance Issues in Grant Seeking

By Michelle Adams

As your nonprofit begins applying for grants, there are several legal aspects to consider. The first logical question concerns the correct legal formation of your organization. A second consideration is the importance of good organizational governance in obtaining grants. Lastly, some key distinctions between seeking private and public grants will be addressed.

Importance of Proper Formation

Many grant proposals stipulate that your nonprofit must be "properly formed." They will request your organization's constitutional documents reflecting this requirement.

Tax-Exemption. The vast majority of private and public grantors require grant recipients to be tax-exempt nonprofits. They will often ask for a copy of the Letter of Determination from the IRS to demonstrate this. The tax-exempt status is important to the grantor for several reasons. First, since the organizations giving the grants are tax-exempt entities themselves, their dollars must be used to further tax-exempt purposes. If the money is not given to an IRS-recognized charity, there is a much greater administrative burden to ensure the money is used properly. If a private foundation grants money to an organization that does not fall into this category, it becomes responsible for administering ongoing expenditure responsibility,[5] which means that it must oversee, verify, and document that the money was used for charitable purposes.

Organizational Form. Tax-exempt organizations can take the form of nonprofit corporations, charitable trusts, or more recently, LLCs. It frequently makes a difference whether the nonprofit is a charitable organization or another type of tax-exempt organization (there are dozens). Some government grants are only available to the former.[6] Private foundations are required to distribute only to public charities as described in 509(a)(1), (2), or (3).

Internal Restrictions. Your organization must make sure that your governing documents do not prohibit you from seeking and receiving grants from certain kinds of organizations.

International Charities Seeking U.S. Grants. If you are an international charity seeking U.S. grants, it is advisable to pursue IRS tax exemption recognition. Private foundations are often reluctant to make international grants to unrecognized entities as it would normally require them to exercise the aforementioned expenditure responsibility (which may be difficult to administer given the geographical considerations). Alternately, the donor can make what is called an "equivalency determination."[7] This means that the granting foundation has made a good faith determination that the foreign charity is the equivalent of a U.S. public charity.[8]

Either of these options necessitates further actions on the part of the grantor which may bias a decision against your organization.

Since September 11, 2001 there is regulatory push to tighten donations to foreign organizations in an effort to prevent money from ultimately ending up in the wrong hands.[9] Recently, measures taken towards greater accountability and transparency among charities in general has resulted in greater scrutiny of international grant making.

There are two options for foreign charities to obtain recognition by the IRS. You can apply directly for recognition as a foreign 501(c)(3) charity, but this only carries benefits for organizational grants, not for individual donors. Since individual donations are often expected and no tax deduction accrues to the donor under this approach, this option is rarely employed.

The other option is to establish a separate 501(c)(3) public charity in the United States, allowing it to raise funds, and then make grants back to the foreign charity. This requires the extra effort of establishing and managing a nonprofit entity, but this scenario affords the domestic entity the same advantages as any other U.S. charity – including the ability to offer income tax deductions for its individual donors.

Importance of Good Governance

The IRS believes that "a well-governed charity is more likely to obey the tax laws, safeguard charitable assets, and serve charitable interests than one with poor or lax governance."[10] Few "best practices" of nonprofit governance are codified in the law—and yet they are considered vitally important to the basic health of an organization. Also, these practices will usually be an area of inquiry by grantors who will want assurance that the funds will be handled in a responsible, effective, and efficient manner.

In 2007, the IRS published a list of what it considers to be good governance practices.[11] The list has since been removed from the IRS website as the revised Form 990 has incorporated these concepts, but the list still provides guidance on what the IRS and the philanthropic community expects in terms of best practices. Several topics from that list and associated recommendations are discussed below.

Strong Mission Statement. The first item mentioned in the publication was a "strong mission statement." In the context of grant seeking, your organization's mission statement needs to be specific, compelling, and feasible. It serves both to popularize and explain the existence of your organization.

Grantors will be looking for evidence of sound strategic planning and a demonstrated record of success in your organization's focus area. This focus must be in line with the aim of the granting organization. Every grant seeking organization must also guard against "mission creep" – allowing the focus of your organization to morph by pursuing grants that are available but do not align with your mission. Your governing board should make periodic reviews of your vision and mission statement to stay on track.

Ethics. Develop a written Code of Ethics to demonstrate a commitment to legal and ethical integrity. Include a Whistleblower Policy to protect employees that choose to reveal their good faith suspicions of inappropriate or illegal behavior within the organization. The 2002 Sarbanes-Oxley Act, although created in response to for-profit entities, fueled the trend towards an expectation of whistleblower policies in all types of entities. In fact, the revised Form 990 for the tax year 2008 asks nonprofits to reveal whether they have such a policy in place.

While private schools are required to have a racially non-discriminatory policy to be tax exempt, most organizations applying for grants – schools or otherwise – will also be asked to produce a non-discriminatory policy or to include a statement affirming that they follow such a practice. Some applications will specify the type of policy they are looking for, such as the process for hiring employees, selecting clients, and providing services. The basis upon which the discrimination policy applies, such as race, religion, gender, national origin, age, medical condition, disability, veteran status, marital status, sexual orientation, or any other characteristic protected by law, may be requested. Although such a policy is not required by law, the fact that most grant applications request it and that the IRS asks about it on the publically viewable Form 990 makes it important that you adopt an appropriate one.

Due Diligence. Another necessary aspect is due diligence on your leadership's part. Board members should act in good faith like any prudent person would in a similar position. Both the IRS and grantors are interested in seeing that your board has policies to promote due diligence. Make sure each of your directors are familiar with your activities and know whether those activities promote your mission and achieve its goals, that each director is fully informed about your financial status, and that each has full and accurate information to make informed decisions. Among other questions that probe levels of communication and involvement, many grant applications inquire about the level of commitment and advocacy on the board, the qualifications for leadership, and the frequency of board meetings.

Duty of Loyalty. Your directors should act in the best interest of your organization, demonstrating what is termed "duty of loyalty." Neither board directors nor key employees may benefit from your charity doing business with an entity in which they have an interest. If someone in the organization stands to benefit from a transaction with the organization, it must be scrutinized carefully. It must be exposed early on for the rest of the board to vote upon in the absence of the interested director. The transaction must actually be advantageous to the charity, and not a worse deal than could be obtained on the open market.

The increasing importance of independent[12] board members grows clear. Lois G. Lerner, director of the exempt-organization division of the IRS, said, "While the IRS cannot require groups to have a conflict-of-interest policy or independent board members, the lack of those policies could trigger other questions about how a nonprofit organization would prevent abuses and insider dealing."[13] Boards composed entirely of family members are also disfavored;[14] some states even do not allow it.[15] Such boards are perceived as more prone to serve the interests of the family rather than the organization as a whole.

This quest for board independence and accountability is what motivates grantors to ask about such things as your organization's policy on length of board terms. They will inquire into the identity of your board members, their employers, areas of expertise, and relations to the staff – professional and familial.

Compensation Practices. Another facet of good governance is the prohibition against private gain.[16] The charity does not exist for the benefit of private individuals. Compensation for employees and directors, as well as reimbursement policies, is considered when evaluating policies. Your organization should always be able to demonstrate how a salary figure was established. Document your research with similar positions in the nonprofit and for-profit world.[17] Soaring salaries for nonprofit executives is no longer being ignored.

The salaries of top employees are publically available on the charity's Form 990. Charities should have a reimbursement policy in place, more as a response to misinformation than for prevention of intentional abuse. IRS rules in this area are more clearly set forth than in many related governance areas, but these rules are largely ignored in many church and charity circles. Without clear policies and consistent practices in this area, both your charity and affected individuals are subject to penal actions on the part of the IRS.

Transparency and Financial Audits. Grant applications commonly require evidence of financial transparency and accountability. With the advent of the revised Form 990 in tax year 2008, charities are being pushed to display greater transparency. This more detailed form can be an opportunity for your charity to showcase its accomplishments, fiscal health, and the strength of its governance policies.

Although small charities may not find independent audits financially feasible, organizations seeking larger donations need to consider them. The U.S. Treasury recommends such an audit when the charity's gross income exceeds $250,000 annually.[18] An audit is mandatory for each year that a federal grant exceeds $500,000.[19]

Diverse Support. Although it is not mentioned in the IRS publication, an important consideration in grant seeking is the level of support for the prospective program. Aside from the need for publically supported charities to meet a required "support test,"[20] regular financial support from diverse sources assures a grantor that your organization has something others have seen and believe in. It also indicates that the programming will have enough support to continue after the grant funding has expired. Grantors desire to see strong constituency support through annual giving and a professional approach to the relationships with major donors.

Contributions personally made by the board as a whole to the organization in each of the last three years is information grantors often require. An organization may also be asked to describe its collaboration efforts with other organizations.

References from reputable individuals and organizations outside the organization speak volumes as well. Obtaining a stamp of approval from organizations such as the Evangelical Council for Financial Accountability is a meaningful benchmark in the world of Christian philanthropy. The governance standards that accompany such recognition require more accountability and transparency than the legal requirements alone or the status quo, and donors are also able to weigh an approved organization's effectiveness in terms of dollars spent on administration versus actual program work through publically available data.

Other Grant-Associated Legal Obligations

Certain governance practices become requisite when an organization accepts a grant. This transaction is the equivalent of entering into a contract with the grantor. An organization can potentially be in breach of contract in the following ways: 1) not using the funds as directed; 2) not reporting back to the grantor of the funds as required; and 3) not returning surplus funds if that is stipulated.

Charities applying for and receiving grants may be required to register in the state where they are applying. Charitable Solicitation Registration (CSR) laws exist in most states and on some local levels as well. Some CSR laws specifically include grant seeking as an activity requiring registration (before seeking charitable gifts in locations with these laws, a charity must register itself – regardless of whether the gift is ultimately received).[21] Some exclude certain kinds of grant seeking, such as government grants.[22] Because of the diversity of requirements, it is important to investigate the

CSR laws in each location where your organization plans to request funds. Fines have been imposed when charities have ignored these regulations.[23]

Government Grants

The federal government awards over $350 billion in grant money each year, but this funding does not come without strings.

Bookkeeping. Your organization should be aware that government grants are accompanied by increased paperwork. This can include certifications, budget reports, and other reporting documentation to prove that your organization's programs are staying on task in meeting objectives and using designated funds appropriately. For federal grants, financial reporting is done on Standard Form 269. In the case of a federal grant, an audit can be performed at any time, making accurate bookkeeping vitally important. As stated earlier, an audit is mandatory for each year that the federal grant exceeds $500,000.

Governance. Certain governance issues can develop when accepting government funding. Dependence upon these grants is a real temptation for many charities, resulting in the aforementioned *mission creep* where the original purpose of the organization changes to chase the available funds. Government grants often require matching funds, something your organization needs to consider before applying for the grant. Funding from another government grant will not constitute matching funds in fulfillment of this requirement.

If your organization is considering using part of its funds for political activity, it should seek private rather than government funding and make certain it is properly structured to engage in such activity.[24] By law, federal funds may not be used for lobbying.

In addition to governance and extensive reporting issues, constitutionality is an important consideration when accepting government money. Because the Establishment Clause prevents the government from advancing or inhibiting any religion, government funds cannot be used to support religious activities.[25]

In two major cases in recent years, the actions of religious organizations in accepting government grants were declared to be unconstitutional.[26]

Although neither faith-based organization was ultimately required to return the funds that were issued prior to the declaration of unconstitutionality, the penultimate court in each case had ordered that the entire grant be repaid – including funds which had long been spent.

Simply because a government entity bestows a grant does not mean that it was constitutionally done. It is not enough to rely upon the giver of a grant to know the constitutional boundaries; your organization must be proactive in evaluating the situation before accepting the money to avoid a potentially expensive lawsuit and disruption of your plans. Secondly, although the cited organizations were not forced to return grant money that had already been disseminated, it is not possible to rely on this precedent for future cases. If the *Flast v. Cohen* case is ever expanded beyond its narrow facts (as the lower courts attempted to do), it could change the results for other faith-based organizations that accept government grants.

Thirdly, it is imperative that faith-based organizations keep very strict and separate accounts when accepting government funds so if a lawsuit would accuse you of spending significant portions for religious purposes, your organization will have a defense. You will have a better defense if you can show that all the funding supporting religious activities or materials comes solely from private sources. Have employees keep a log of religious and nonreligious hours spent. As scrutiny increases upon faith-based organizations, accepting government funding will call for the highest standards of record keeping and integrity.

The goal of any grant applicant, private or public, is to stand out among other seekers. Going above and beyond in terms of the above cited best practices will help accomplish that and will also push your charity to an even greater level of organizational excellence.

~~~

Michelle A. Adams is an attorney in Augusta, Georgia specializing in nonprofit law. She focuses on guiding new Christian ministries through the organization and tax exemption process. She has experience in grant writing, grant reviewing, and advising grantmaking institutions – particularly in the area of international grants. She is an active trustee on the board for Thembalitsha USA which makes grants to support humanitarian efforts in Africa. Michelle received her B.A. from Cedarville University and J.D. from Regent University School of Law.
~~~

Chapter 6

Perspectives from the Grant Maker and Grant Writer

By Gene Rietfors

The first time I sat face-to-face with a foundation officer—I hoped to receive a grant for the organization I represented as development director—I found myself growing more and more uncomfortable as his questions moved from inquiry to interrogation. I contemplated how much easier life might be on "the other side," his side, of the table.

Some years later, while actually working on "the other side," I discovered that life was indeed different, but not necessarily easier. There was a never-ending flow of proposals to review and analyze, a great deal of diligence required, a steady line of grant seekers wanting to be seen, projects to be monitored, and a Board of Trustees whose questions of my recommendations sometimes felt more like, well, interrogation. Also, it was never easy to tell an organization that its proposal was denied, especially when I had recommended it to my Board for funding.

I developed an eye for grant proposals that were most likely to find favor with my foundation board. Some were not the best written proposals, but if I felt the projects fit our guidelines and were worthy of consideration, I would occasionally help a prospective grantee rework a proposal. I tried to treat the person on the other side of the table as I would want to be treated. I reminded myself that both of us sought an outcome that would honor my foundation's mission as well as serve the other person's organization's best interests.

Now that I am back on the "asking side" of philanthropy, I occasionally write grant proposals. The job hasn't gotten any easier, but it helps to study the work of other successful writers and to remember the things I looked for when I was reviewing and analyzing proposals that were on their way toward approval (or denial). What follows are some things I learned on "both sides of the table," although my main focus will be on the grant writer's side.

Don't Just Read the Guidelines – Get to Know Them

I worked for a large foundation that has very specific guidelines: it supports programs devoted to Christian evangelism. The foundation keeps a low profile, but its guidelines are readily available to any organization requesting them. It was surprising to see the number of proposals – and the organizations submitting them – that did not come even close to matching our stated mission and interests. Of all the proposals I read, none was farther off the mark than a request from a zoo in upstate New York. The zoo asked for money to purchase an elephant. I really had to restrain myself when I wrote the letter of denial.

Information about foundations' interests and funding patterns are readily available from a number of sources. However, it is best to check directly with the foundation before you submit a proposal.

It's also important to remain updated on the foundation's interests. Its mission and guidelines probably will not change, but its priorities – a specific problem to be addressed, for example, or a particular geographic focus – may vary from year to year. This is especially true of foundations that fund projects nationally or internationally.

Getting to Know the Funders

Foundations, like individuals, have their own personalities and funding passions. Whether with foundations or with individual donors, good relationships are always helpful. It is still true that people give to people.

If you do not have a relationship or much familiarity with a foundation, submitting a full proposal isn't usually the best way to begin a relationship. Most foundation staff members are open to phone calls or letters of inquiry.

It really helps to request a personal meeting with a foundation officer – but only after you are convinced that your organization and your project will be a good fit with the foundation. Almost all – maybe 99 percent – of the organizations receiving grants while I was a program officer were those with whom I'd had one or more personal meetings. While not all foundation staff will be this approachable, since I had experienced life on the "asking side," I tried to be as accessible as possible.

A colleague at another foundation once told me, "About 75 to 80 percent of our grants are to organizations that we have given to in the past." He described his foundation's relationships with grantees as much like the dating process: starting off slow, to see what works and what doesn't. Sometimes it can take years before a foundation is truly comfortable with an organization, and vice-versa. As the grantee, your role in the relationship is determined largely by your integrity, transparency, and credibility – doing what you say you'll do and accomplishing the goals you set.

There's no shortage of good organizations with good projects. Foundations strive to sort out the better projects from the good ones and then *invest in the best.*

Crafting the Proposal

It can't be overstated: know the foundation's guidelines. Even if a letter of inquiry isn't stipulated, it is advisable to send one before submitting a full proposal. That letter is your "two-minute elevator speech" designed to grab the readers' attention and compel them to want to know more.

Some foundations require proposals to conform to their own application template – if so, follow it! (You won't have a choice if the proposal has to be submitted online at the foundation's website.) If the foundation specifies a maximum length for proposals, don't exceed that length. (Some foundations simply toss out pages that exceed their stated maximum.) If you can tell your story effectively in fewer pages than the maximum allowed, so much the better.

Besides following template guidelines, there are several other tips I've discovered make proposals more presentable and credible.

Unless you are instructed to use them, hard covers are unnecessary. I found it was difficult to file proposals that arrived in hardcover folders or notebooks, so I always discarded the covers.

Proposals don't need to be slick, four-color sales brochures, but that doesn't mean they aren't selling your project or organization to a grant maker. A well-written, well-articulated proposal will command attention. Your proposal should use a readable type font, utilize subheads and bullets, and employ adequate white space. It's acceptable to use boxes to highlight important statements and quotes. Also, photos, illustrations, and anecdotes, if they make a case, can add sizzle. Finally, compelling, brief human interest stories capture a program's excitement and impact.

Budget calculations and statistics must be accurate. A proposal should be proofread by more than one set of eyes to make sure that all the numbers add up and to ensure there are no spelling or grammatical errors. A computer's spell check doesn't know when to use "its" or "it's," and it cannot tell the difference between "affect" and "effect." There may be other folks like me who are uncharitable when it comes to misspelled words, improper punctuation, and bad grammar.

The amount of a request needs to be adequate but logical. When I was reviewing proposals, red flags went up whenever a group sought a grant that was disproportionate to its annual revenue. For example, an organization with a $200,000 yearly budget might request a $150,000 grant. It's clear that they failed to realize such a large and immediate infusion of money could produce more harm than good. The amount was simply beyond the organization's capacity to manage effectively and prudently.

Foundations pay attention to an organization's program and project goals, and once they invest money, they expect to see how the results match the goals. This underscores how important it is for a proposal to show how a project's outcomes can and will be measured. Some foundations may suggest that proposals include logic models (inputs, activities, outputs, results) to measure a project's impact.

After the Grant Is Made

Foundations—and most individuals, for that matter—don't give money without establishing reporting requirements. As thorough as you are in preparing and presenting proposals, you need to be just as conscientious in reporting results and accounting for the grant money spent on your project.

When I served with the foundation, I was surprised and disappointed at the number of times grantees had to be reminded that their reports were overdue. Even more troubling was when an organization spent grant money for purposes not designated in their original proposal. That happened twice during my time at the foundation. In one instance, the organization was a victim of circumstances it couldn't control; the other time was a case of misunderstanding. Both organizations apologized profusely and voluntarily returned their entire grant. Our board later reissued the funds in recognition of the organizations' willingness to give up money rather than their credibility.

Many foundations want to see firsthand the projects they fund. Site visits can be great opportunities for you to display your organization's capacity and capability to earn future program support. The visits I made often revealed additional funding opportunities for our foundation.

When the Grant Maker Says "No"

A few foundations may reject the first proposal from an organization they have never supported. Many times, however, "no" also means "try us again." In my own grantmaking experience, some organizations presented two or three proposals to us before submitting one that resulted in a grant.

There's no stigma to a denial; in fact, it is often to an organization's credit when it continues to seek for programs that come closest to matching the foundation's priorities. Finally, whenever I was asked, I did my best to explain why an organization's proposal was denied. Most foundations will do the same.

A Few More Observations

- Foundations are rarely sources of ongoing operating funds. Most prefer to make one-time or limited-time grants for specific programs or projects. Some will fund capacity building needs, but these also tend to be one-time grants.
- Some foundations will make multi-year grants, and usually in annually declining amounts. The foundation I served might make a tentative, non-binding commitment for two or three years, but the grantee was required to reapply each year.
- Many foundations are receptive to matching or challenge grant proposals. A few require the organization to raise a matching amount before they release their funds. Try to be fairly sure at the time your proposal is submitted that your organization will be able to meet the matching challenge.
- If a proposal calls for collaborating with other organizations, it's important to have the collaboration in place before the proposal is submitted.
- A proposal that says – or even implies – that an organization is desperate for money ("We may have to close our doors if we don't receive a grant") will probably be denied. Foundations aren't anxious to rescue sinking organizations.
- Once your proposal is submitted, prepare to wait. Some foundations make grants monthly, and others give quarterly or annually. A few don't have giving schedules. It can take months between the time a proposal is received and a grant is made. A quick decision on a proposal usually means a denial – the request didn't make the "first cut."
- Lobbying can damage your chances for a grant. Once in a while, someone – usually the organization's

executive director – would call one of our foundation's trustees, seeking favor for a pending proposal. As often as not, the trustee wouldn't be familiar with the proposal (since it hadn't been presented to the full board), and furthermore, resented being contacted at all. And such lobbying doesn't set well with foundation staff either.

- Don't propose a project solely for the purpose of satisfying a foundation's priorities and interests. Even if your proposal is successful, you'll eventually be saddled with funding a program that doesn't fit *your* priorities.
- Don't overlook the way you present yourself. Regardless of the foundation's dress code, you can't go wrong by wearing business attire – even if the foundation folks are in casual dress. This means coat and tie for men, appropriate suit or dress for women.

And Finally. . .

Every so often someone asks me, "Which is the preferred role—grant maker or grant seeker?" Each has its unique rewards and challenges, and both play an important part in meeting the needs of people. It doesn't really matter as long as you're comfortable on your side of the table.

~~~

Gene Rietfors has degrees from Colorado State University (B.A. Journalism) and Michigan State University (M.A. Continuing Education). He served as vice president and then as president of the Harry J. Lloyd Charitable Trust. He directed the development programs for Baker University and for the Salvation Army in Kansas City and Detroit. Most
~~~

recently, he was the manager of development and communications for the Kansas City Rescue Mission. He has experience in grant making and grant seeking. He has written successful proposals and appeal letters for several nonprofits in Kansas City.

Chapter 7

The Professional Grant Writer

By Joyce A. Leggette

Hiring a professional grant writer is a major decision for any nonprofit because the professional detail the writer provides may determine the success or failure of your proposal. Well-established nonprofits often have full-time employees dedicated to fundraising, grant writing, and community relations. However, many new and growing organizations have some questions related to grant writers.

This chapter is dedicated to both the new organization and to the growing organization with a small budget that wants to expand its revenue by including annual grants. In this section, some common questions are addressed: How do you know when to hire a professional grant writer? How do you know what to reasonably expect and how much to pay the grant writer? What information should you give the grant writer so they can do a good job for you? Should you have a contract with the writer? Does a professional grant writer solve all of your funding concerns? If not, then why not?

When to Hire a Professional Grant Writer

In many organizations, the real question is "when," not "if," although the "if" may transpire in some ministries. In short, you are ready to hire a grant writer when you have prepared all of the supporting documents the writer needs to do a good job. If you hire a professional grant writer before preparing your supporting documents, you waste time and add substantial fees to the writer's bill.

Below is a list of supporting documents you should collect before soliciting a grant writer's services:

- A professionally written business plan (typically 20-25 pages).
- An executive summary for your organization (include a mission and a vision statement).
- The cash flow, profit and loss statement, and the monthly statements of your organization for the last 3-5 years (one year of statements if you are a new company). It should be professionally prepared by your staff accountant or CPA, saved in a standard format in Excel or QuickBooks, and mailed to your grant writer
- The organization's legal papers (include copies of legal documents, by-laws, etc.).
- Copies of your IRS 501(c)3.
- Copies of your IRS tax ID papers..
- Copies of your organization's IRS tax returns for the last 3 years
- Copies of your state tax numbers.
- Copies of your minority status papers (if applicable).
- A collection of JPEG (picture) files on a CD; these photos should include everything from professional

pictures of your board members to your office or your organization in action in your community.
- A one paragraph qualifications summary on each board member (each summary should not exceed 200 words).

All documents should be saved on a CD in Microsoft Word for the writer to edit, rewrite, and manipulate. There should be at least two clean copies of state or federal papers (tax papers, etc.) in a cardboard folder that are mailed along with the CD.

Frequently, organizations have every document except the business plan. A good grant writer can also prepare a business plan depending on the size and age of your organization and the complexity of your organization's details. If your grant writer needs to prepare your business plan, be ready to meet with him or her for up to two hours. Allow the writer an additional two weeks to write it, depending on the writer's project schedule.

Once you have these documents prepared and collected, then you are ready to contact a professional grant writer.

Grant Timelines & What to Expect From the Writer

First, expect professionalism. While some people think professionalism entails hand-holding and constant reassurance, this reduces productivity and profits. So, if your grant writer does not want to spend the entire afternoon on the phone with you talking about everything imaginable, understand that excessive phone time is a loss of production and revenue for a professional writer. However, you should expect politeness.

Also, expect directness: the writer should give you a list of exactly what is needed from you. Expect to spend 30 minutes to an hour talking with the writer to give him or her a feel for your organization, and then expect the writer to do as promised.

The grant writer should give you a timing outline for the grant process. This is a two-way process: the writer needs information *from* you in order to accurately prepare an outline for you. The writer also needs to see the grant or foundation information related to your potential source of funding before making any timing estimates for you.

It is detrimental to everyone involved for you to approach a professional grant writer as the savior for your ministry. Often linked with the "save me" cry is the unrealistic idea of normal grant funding timelines. It is very rare to apply for a grant within 30 days of obtaining a grant writer, or to receive funding less than 6 months after you begin working with your writer. Occasionally, you will find a foundation or grant opportunity that has an application deadline within 30 days of when you discovered it, but more often, the application deadline is still months away. Once the grant deadline passes, it usually takes two to six months before the grant is funded if your organization is awarded the grant.

It is best to allow the grant writer three to four months of preparation time *prior to the application deadline*. The exception to this general rule is if the application is online. However, the grant writer still needs at least two months to ensure supporting documents are properly prepared and in order. Remember, a good grant writer will customize your documents [i.e. edit accordingly] for each grant application.

Editing and customizing an application is a process that requires time. Keep in mind that professional grant writers usually have multiple clients and projects. So, while your ministry's proposal may take only a few weeks to prepare, you should allow for more time because of the writer's other obligations (unless the writer's time is totally dedicated to your project).

If you have done the prerequisite research to identify funding sources, the writer can begin work immediately on your grant proposals. If you have not researched which grants your organization qualifies for, when their applications are due, what they fund, and what each of them requires, etc., you can do the research or pay the writer to research. However, it is best to finish researching before contacting grant writers.

If your grant writer needs to do the research, set aside an additional $500 to $1,500 for online access fees and the researcher's time. These larger databases for research can cost $179 or more per month just for access to their data. This is important to remember, especially if you want your grant writer to complete your research. Since the grant writer does the research for you, it is both reasonable and fair for you to pay these access fees.

Finally, the grant writer should prepare a contract in which he or she outlines the deliverables and timeline that was agreed upon by both parties. The contract should include a fee payment schedule in which you agree to pay as the deliverables are met. Writers who present themselves as professional grant writers but don't expect you to sign a contract should be avoided. If the writer does not commit in writing to deliverables and dates, then your organization will probably not meet the grant submission deadlines.

Payments: Fair and Reasonable

On the Internet, it is possible to find everything from $5,000 grant writing quotes to promises that your organization will be funded if a particular group writes your grant proposal.

Grant writers should not have to "prove themselves" by writing without pay unless the grant is won. A professional grant writer provides professional writing, but does not make or break your application. (See the next section for more information on this topic.)

If you contract a secular grant writer, you can reasonably expect to pay the full fee up front. If you choose a non-traditional or Christian grant writer, then you can expect to pay according to the contract.

The Writer's Limitations

As indicated in the previous section, there are limitations to the grant writer's ability to win funding. First and foremost, you should never expect a grant writer to promise that you will win a grant. This is patently unfair and ridiculous.

This example illustrates this concept: the Ford Foundation is one of the largest foundations in the United States today and it distributes enormous amounts of funding across the world. However, only 4.5% of the grant applications Ford receives each year actually win funding.[27]

This also explains why a professional grant writer cannot reasonably agree to be paid only if you win the grant. If you were to ask your grant writer to submit to Ford Foundation with the agreement to be paid only if you won funding, then that would essentially be an agreement to work for free since there is a mere 4.5% chance of getting paid. The writer has no control over the foundation's decision-making process or how many other organizations will compete with yours for foundation grants.

Other circumstances the grant writer cannot affect include foundation decisions to discontinue funding, new limitations on who can apply, the sales content of your proposal, the accuracy of your included financials, your ministry's lack of longevity, the lack of experience of your executive director or board members, a poor reputation in the community, recent financial fraud committed with foundation money, or any number of other factors can move your organization down on the funding list or can break the deal completely.

Your professional grant writer's job is to make your organization look smart, organized, effective, and like a worthwhile effort in which a foundation should invest. Remember, the grant writer's primary job is to write with excellence.

~~~

Joyce A. Leggette, Ph.D. is the senior editor and publisher at Shulamite Publishing House based in Southlake, Texas. As a born-again Christian since 1975, with an undergraduate degree in English and minor in religion, she brings more than 20 years of professional writing experience to the grant writing process. She has written grants for nonprofit organizations, both as a staff fundraiser and as a freelancer, since 1991.
~~~

Chapter 8

Writing the Grant Proposal

By Gil Mertz

After you have researched and contacted foundations, your success is determined by your written grant proposal. First, it is crucial that you understand the competition for foundation dollars. Requests far exceed available funds and the default position of most foundations is to look for reasons to decline your grant proposal. Your proposal must stand out in order for your request to be funded.

Common Mistakes

Avoid these mistakes regularly found in grant proposals.

Failure to Follow Instructions. Most foundations provide instructions or guidelines either online or by mail. It is extremely important that you follow these instructions exactly. What use is a 20-page grant proposal if the foundation specifically gave you a five-page limit?

Assumption of Reader Knowledge. Don't assume too much when explaining a project or program you hope to fund.

It is easy to assume others know what you are talking about because you work so closely with the project. However, you must assume that the foundation knows absolutely nothing about you, your program, or your organization.

Exchange of Quantity for Quality. A long proposal is not necessarily a good proposal. As you write, put yourself in the place of the person who will read your proposal—and dozens more—this week. Don't overwhelm him or her with reams of paper; make yours stand out with quality, concise information.

Assumption That the Grant Is About You. Avoid the common misconception that grants are about you, your needs, or your organization. This is backwards thinking. Foundations give grants not because they can extend *your* vision, but because you can extend *their* vision. They are in the business of giving money to causes that are important to *them*. The better you communicate how your organization can help extend *their* vision by speaking *their* language and matching *their* passions, the better your chances are for receiving a grant.

Components of the Grant Proposal

Although grant proposals appear in many forms, the following elements should be included in most proposals.

Title. Do not underestimate the importance of this small item. Most grant reviewers decide within seconds whether to continue reading or to put your request into the decline folder. What can you say in one line that sets your grant proposal apart from the others competing for the same foundation dollars?

Your title should express action, be specific, offer a promise, and use the same language as that of the foundation. For example, instead of the generic proposal title, "Serving the Health Needs of the Poor," a better title would be "Increasing Services to Low-Income Families by Expanding Our Medical Clinic." Look for key buzz words on the foundation's website or in its guidelines. If the foundation uses the term "low-income families," work that phrase into your title.

Executive Summary. It is refreshing for the grant reviewer to find a summary of your request at the front instead of wading through pages of content. This summary is incredibly important because it is the sales pitch of your proposal—it convinces the reader the proposal is worth the time it takes to read.

In this summary, you provide a brief statement describing the need, a proposal describing how your organization can provide the solution, and your specific request which includes the grant amount. This should not exceed one page.

Your summary, like the title, should speak the same language as that of the foundation. It should do more than just represent a project you think the foundation would support; it should borrow the same words and phrases the foundation uses to describe its funding interests. Consider writing this section last.

Statement of Need. Remember that need is not based on what you want as an organization; it is based on the need in your community. In other words, your organization might need new computers for your after-school program, but *the* need is not computers for your organization. The need is the fact that children in your community are falling behind acceptable academic levels in school due to poverty, gang activity, low parental involvement, or any array of other issues.

In this case, present the need of children who are struggling in school and your responsibility to help them through tutoring and other resources. However, adding six computers for your after-school outreach is an important part of that program. The *project* is purchasing new computers, but the *need* is helping students who are falling behind academically.

Independent research and facts are the best way to substantiate need. The Internet is an inexhaustible source of studies, facts, statistics, and data that will support your cause. Remember to use up-to-date reports and identify your sources. For example, do not just say that juvenile delinquency is on the rise in local schools. Say instead, "In 2007, the Los Angeles School Board reported that juvenile delinquency increased by 19% over the past year."

Do not overwhelm the reader with endless statistics; use only those which best illustrate the need. Educate the foundation regarding the current issue and demonstrate that your organization is fully informed and prepared to address the need. Bulleted points will help your statistics stand out.

<u>Solution</u>. Your next step is to demonstrate that your organization is prepared and qualified to meet the need you described. Although you will discuss your specific project in the following section, this section gives the foundation a general overview of your organization. However, this is not a detailed résumé with a complete history—you can enclose a brochure or direct the reader to your website for that purpose.

In less than one page, relate when and how your organization was established, your mission statement, your expertise, your overall programs, the demographics and quantity of people you assist, any collaboration with other organizations, and some highlights from your organization's accomplishments.

It is imperative that you demonstrate how your organization is distinctive from similar organizations. Is any other organization doing what you are doing? What makes you different? Are you the largest or only agency in your field for your particular geographic area or specific people group? Foundations do not encourage duplication.

Project Description. Most foundations require five basic elements in a grant proposal: objectives, methods, staffing, evaluation, and sustainability. You have already described the problem/need and how your agency is meeting this need. Now, be more specific about your grant request. Start by repeating the title and a line or two about the project from the executive summary, and then describe your objectives.

Objectives. Objectives are the measurable outcomes of the program. Your objectives must be specific, tangible, attainable, and measurable. For example, if you wish to help students who are performing poorly in school, you cannot only say you want to help them do better. Instead, your objectives might look like this:

- Each student will improve reading comprehension to at least a C level.
- Each student will read one book per quarter for the next school semester.
- Each student will increase his or her math score to a passing level or by ten percentage points by the end of the school year.
- Each student will demonstrate the five responsible uses of the Internet for school projects.
- No student will be absent from school more than two days per semester.

Methods. Methods describe how you plan to meet your objectives. Who will do this, where will it happen, when will it be done, and how will it be executed? Write about your staff and volunteers, your facility, when you meet, your specific programs, what happens during your programs, how many people you reach, any collaborations with other organizations, and what makes your program unique.

Staffing. Explain who runs your project and their qualifications. Foundations want to know they are investing in programs and projects led by quality people with special training. They also want to know if your organization engages volunteers from the community whenever appropriate.

Evaluation. Foundations want to know what accountability you have to ensure everything you promised will be accomplished. How can you assure them that what you say will happen? What systems are in place to evaluate if this is a good program? What does success look like?

In our example of helping students who perform poorly in school, you could substantiate your accomplishments with the actual student report cards, school attendance records, meetings with school teachers, and consultations with parents. You must find ways to document the results of your project and report them back to the foundation. Although the foundation wants to see success, it is more important to receive honest feedback.

Sustainability. The final issue to address is how the program or project will continue after the grant is spent. You may be required to list other sources and amounts of funding obtained and expected sources of continued funding. Foundations do not want to give grants for a program that has to end when the grant expires. Do not only list other grants; mention all sources of income, including individuals, churches, corporations, events, and other revenue streams that support your project.

Grant Request. Summarize your proposal in one or two concluding paragraphs. Make a final appeal for your project and add the specific amount of the grant you request. Briefly reiterate what your organization wants to do and why it is important. Offer your contact information in case the foundation has any questions, would like more information, or would like to make a site visit. Close by thanking them for considering your grant request.

Attachments. Every foundation will require attachments. Clip these together in a separate group from the grant proposal. Read and follow the instructions carefully. You may be required to supply multiple copies of certain documents or not to staple other documents. Send only the requested attachments. Most foundations request the following documents:

- Copy of your 501(c)(3) federal tax-exemption letter (Some foundations may require a similar tax-exemption letter from your state.).
- List of your board of directors and their business affiliations.
- Copy of your operational budget.
- Copy of the specific project budget.
- Most recent financial audit.
- Copy of your IRS Form 990.
- Copy of your annual report.
- Biographies of key staff.
- Endorsements.
- Promotional materials, such as brochures and DVDs.

Before You Mail It

Check the deadline to ensure you mail or deliver the grant proposal in time.

Add a one-page and highly personalized cover letter on your letterhead. Summarize your grant request; you can use content from your executive summary. State the amount of the grant you are seeking.

Double check to make sure you answered all questions and that you are sending all required materials. Make a copy of the proposal for your files; foundations often call back with specific questions. Proofread everything; proofread again. Pray.

After You Mail It

Approximately one week after submitting your grant proposal, call to make sure that it arrived and that it is complete. Inform the foundation by letter if you have major successes with the project, media coverage, or grants from other sources during the review period which can take one to six months. While you await a decision, repeat the grant proposal process with other foundations.

If your proposal is declined, send a letter to thank the foundation for considering your request. Follow up with a phone call to ask why you were declined and what you could do differently the next time you submit a proposal. If you are awarded a grant, send a personal thank you with a receipt. Follow up with a written report after six months and again after one full year.

If you receive more than one grant for the same project and the project is over-funded, request that the second grant be used for a similar project, but offer to send the grant back. With rare exceptions, foundations will allow you to apply the second grant to another project.

Grant writing is a detailed process, but it does not need to be a difficult process. Following the recommendations in this chapter will help your grant stand out and increase your funding opportunities.

~~~

Gil Mertz has been writing grant proposals for more than 30 years. During that time he has successfully raised millions of dollars for a wide variety of ministry causes from small $5,000 projects up to $500,000 capital grants. He is a former pastor and has a wealth of experience in all areas of fundraising and development. He teaches workshops for national groups such as Evangelical Development Ministries and also provides ministry consulting and grant writing services.
~~~

Chapter 9

Presenting a Compelling Statement of Need

By Ben Evans

As a Christian grant writer, the prerequisite to every grant proposal is prayer and seeking God's counsel. Then from there, "do all to the glory of God" (1 Corinthians 10:31).

With this information in mind, we will discuss writing a grant proposal's need statement. This general guide covers the style and necessary components for a need statement written for community foundations and other similar entities. Typically, federal grant proposals are more demanding, and due to spatial limitations, I will address the more common types of funding sources.

Prerequisites

Before you begin your need statement, consider these four writing tips: understand your goal, be clear, be concise, and align your project with your abilities.

First, realize that the goal of your need statement is to motivate your prospective funder to act on behalf of your target audience (those who are affected by your issue and will benefit from your project). Grant writing is actually a form of marketing; you are selling your project to the prospective funder. Convince the funder your project is worth supporting. A key point to remember: Funders are "buying" a solution or positive change.

Secondly, your need statement must be clear. For example, if your issue is the school dropout rate, and you say, "Our city has a high dropout rate, which is causing an increase in property-related crimes in our city," the funder could be confused as to whether you are addressing the school dropout rate or property-related crime. Instead, you should say, "This project will address the school dropout rate in our city, because youth dropping out of school is a major source in the rise of property-related crime."

In addition to clarity about your issue/project, you must also be clear in your facts. You should not write "...our county has a huge problem with youth dropping out of school at an increasingly alarming rate...," because it is vague and does not use statistics.

Also, do not use technical jargon, acronyms, or terms particular to your field because people on review committees may not know this language, making your proposal difficult to understand.

If you can't explain your project clearly, a potential funder might question whether you really know the issue you propose to address.

Thirdly, need statements must be concise because funders receive hundreds of requests and do not like being overwhelmed with content or length. Before writing, check the foundation's guidelines (generally 1-2 pages are the maximum length for a need statement).

Finally, your need statement should clearly align with your organization's mission, experience, and capabilities. Funders generally understand what your organization can realistically accomplish. If your project is so immense that it seems hopeless in terms of your organization's ability to accomplish it, potential funders will question the merits of investing in the project.

Writing the Need Statement

After considering the preceding ideas, begin building your need statement around four basic questions:

1) WHO is your target audience?
2) WHAT problem does this need statement address?
3) WHY should this problem be undertaken?
4) What are the BENEFITS of addressing this need now?

When you answer these questions, support them with the most critical element of your need statement—data. There are two types of data: hard data, which is statistical information; and anecdotal data, which is professional opinions, expert viewpoints, or statements from those influenced by your organization—basically anything that is not statistical.

When you do statistical research, there may or may not be statistics for your exact focus area. If you cannot find information, work geographically outward (local, county, state, and so on) until you find statistics that illustrate your particular issue.

One informational resource that is often overlooked is your local nonprofit resource center that issues Requests For Proposals (RFPs), awards grant funding, and manages grants in accordance with state guidelines. Find out if there is an office for your jurisdiction.

Make sure the data you collect is from qualified sources—i.e. the U.S. Census Bureau, State Department of Education, etc., and not from "www.whiz-bang-info.org." Secondly, confirm that the data is the most current available. If you find your data from the Internet, make sure the links to the data are current.

If you do not carefully check the quality of your sources and its date, you may give your prospective funder outdated information. This makes your organization look out of touch and unacquainted with your target issue.

Finally, if a project statistically shows improvement in the reporting periods, I use this phrase to highlight the urgency of the project: "...while statistics show that [the issue] has improved, there is still much more work to be accomplished. We cannot afford to lose the momentum by stopping now..."

Hard Data

As stated earlier, data is one of the most critical elements in your need statement. Below is a brief discussion of the two types of data.

Hard data is statistical information collected from organizations such as the U.S. Census Bureau, the National Institutes of Health, or other leading organizations. For example, demographics are a type of hard data that can be used to set the scene for your project by giving the funder a glimpse of the community you serve.

> *"As of the census of 2000, there were 2,723 people, 1,172 households, and 723 families residing in the city of Crisfield. The racial makeup of the city was 58.54% White, 37.46% African American, 0.40% Native American, 0.51% Asian, 0.04% Pacific Islander, 0.37% from other races, and 2.68% from two or more races. Hispanics or Latinos of any race were 1.65% of the population. There were 1,172 households out of which 30.3% had children under the age of 18 living with them, 32.9% were married*

couples living together, and 25.4% had a female householder with no husband present. In the city, 27.8% of the population was under the age of 18, 8.3% were ages 18 to 24, and 24.5% were from ages 25 to 44."

After you describe your target population and illustrate your issue with statistics and other evidence, explain your issue's source and the benefits that will come from your project. Look at the following example:

Somerset County has the highest incidence and mortality rates for lung and bronchus cancer in the State of Maryland. The 2003 age-adjusted incidence rate for Somerset County is 139.4. This is almost double the state rate (70.8) and the U.S. Seer Rate (60.0). The age-adjusted mortality rate for lung and bronchus cancer for Somerset County is 93.8, which is nearly double the state rate of 57.3 and the U.S. rate of 54.1. Moreover, in just two years (2001-2003), the rate of incidence of lung cancer has risen 9.3% statewide (2008 Maryland Department of Health and Mental Hygiene, Cigarette Restitution Fund Annual Cancer Report), and 4.3% for adults in Somerset County between 2002 and 2006 (2007 Monitoring Changing Tobacco Use Behaviors in Maryland Report).

Cigarette smoking is the predominant cause of lung cancer according to several major government health authorities: "The most important major risk factor for lung cancer (as well as many other cancers) is tobacco use. Cigarette smoking has been established as the predominant cause of lung cancer, and tobacco smoking is estimated to cause 90% of lung cancer in males and 78% of lung cancer in females" (2008 Maryland Department of Health and Mental Hygiene, Cigarette Restitution Fund Annual Cancer Report).

The 2007 "Monitoring Changing Tobacco Use Behaviors in Maryland" report shows that 19.9% of the adult population in Somerset County smokes. This rate has risen almost 2% over the last year, and is greater than the 2000 rate. Simple addition shows that more than one-quarter of the population of Somerset County smoke—a rate that is unacceptable.

At this rate of incidence, 559 people in Somerset County will be diagnosed with lung cancer this year (based on a population estimate of the 2000 U.S. Census). According to the morality rate, nearly all of these newly diagnosed individuals will die.

Given the rates of lung cancer incidence and mortality in our community, statements from the country's foremost authorities on lung cancer and cigarette smoking, and the rise in the number of adult smokers in our community, it is clear that we take decisive action. We must motivate smokers in our community to quit smoking now.

In the Center for Disease Control's "best practices" for health communication intervention programs, they recommend programs that "deliver strategic, culturally appropriate and high-impact messages in sustained and adequately funded campaigns" (Maryland Department of Health & Mental Hygiene 2008 Annual Cancer Report). The project that our organization is proposing is such a program. It is directed towards the local minority community and is designed to make young people aware of the dangers to which they expose themselves by smoking. Through this outreach project, we expect to reach approximately 10% of our city's population, or about 270 people, with an outcome of at least 100 new enrollees into tobacco cessation programs over the grant period.

Anecdotal Data

The second type of data is anecdotal data. Anecdotal data includes personal stories or professional opinions about your issue—basically any information that is not statistical.

However, there are several things to remember when using anecdotal data. First, only use one or two short stories depending on the space permitted by the funder's guidelines. Secondly, do not use extremely emotional statements or stories. Funders are ordinary people, and like most people, they do not like the manipulation often implied in these stories. Finally, do not only rely on anecdotal data.

The following are examples of anecdotal data. This first one I used in a grant proposal:

> *"In the process of recruiting our task force, one staff member had a discussion with V.H., the mother of a young man attracted to alcohol. After hearing about the environmental approach to youth alcoholism, she exclaimed, "It's about time someone came up with a different approach because the current method is not very effective. I am all for it!"*

Secondly, here is an example of an expert opinion:

> *"We cannot forget the almost 150,000 Maryland residents who currently live with one or more cancers or other diseases caused by their smoking, or the estimated 6,800 who die prematurely each year as a result of their smoking[...] Quitting is often not easy, but with free smoking cessation counseling*

available through local health departments and the Statewide 1-800-QUITNOW telephone cessation counseling service, help is always nearby" (John M. Colmers, Secretary, Maryland Department of Health & Mental Hygiene in the 2008 Cigarette Restitution Fund Annual Cancer Report)."

No matter what type of data you use, use it in moderation because too many statistics can confuse a reviewer, and too much anecdotal data can give an unclear picture of your issue.

As you begin writing your need statement, remember these key points: First, seek God's counsel (an essential element)! Second, realize you are selling a solution or positive change for an issue that is the passion of you and your potential funder. Third, present a clear picture of the people that you serve, the issue that you address, and the issue's source. Submit clear and compelling evidence of the issue's effect on your target area and the results you expect from your project. Finally, remember the overarching goal of your need statement—you are creating a picture of your issue and the people it affects in order to motivate your funders to act on behalf of your target audience.

May God bless you in the grant writing process and give you success!

~~~

Ben Evans has been writing grants for seven years. He volunteers as the vice president of a nonprofit organization and as a grant research and procurement employee for a youth services organization. He has written about a quarter of a million dollars worth of grants for organizations that include health outreach programs, teaching English to
~~~

Hispanic populations, technical mini-grants, youth intervention programs, and family-oriented grants from local, state, and federal sources.

Chapter 10

Drafting the Budget

By Maricia Johns

Writing the budget for a grant can be a daunting task. The budget will remind you of dieting. Don't laugh. Remember when you were trying to diet? You didn't think you really ate that much, so you wrote down everything you put into your mouth for a day. You were amazed how all of the little bites added up. It is the same way with a budget—you must be very thorough and write down everything you need to make your project a success. Every item allowed under the grant's funding guidelines must be factored in.

One of the most important things to remember is that your budget must be detailed. When you create a detailed budget by listing everything you need for a successful project, you can eliminate surprises. You may even remove some items from the budget that are not cost-effective. In addition, detailed budgets are vital because funders do not like surprises—be sure the budget lists every expense mentioned elsewhere in your proposal.

A budget must be as detailed as the funder requires. Some donors, such as the federal government, are extremely detailed, while others are more lenient.

It is essential that you follow the funder's directions. Usually the grant application will provide a budget form with instructions—follow these directions exactly. Now is not the time to show creativity.

As you begin writing your budget, keep the following tips in mind:

First, depending upon the source of the grant, it is helpful to gather this information:

- Payroll Figures
- Surveys
- Marketing
- Staffing Cost
- Tax Returns

Make sure that you know exactly what the donor funds. For example, some donors do not fund salaries, but others consider salaries to be direct costs. However, if you hire grant writers, you cannot pay them a percentage of the awarded grant because their salary is ineligible for funding.

Don't include ineligible costs in your budget even if you think you can demonstrate the necessity of these expenses. This only blemishes your proposal and may cause the reviewer to immediately reject your project.

Next, determine whether your project will be supported by grant funds or a matching project. While it is tempting to ask for finances for your entire project, every donor has funding restrictions. Also, some donors will expect your project to be partially supported by matching funds. Discuss with your donor how much should be matched.

Although your budget will be an estimated number, do not guess—guesses are generally too low or too high. The reviewers are not novices; they can usually spot budgets where the writers guess. However, budgets can be a researched estimate.

Remember that you cannot exceed the total amount for the grant, nor can you ask for more funding if you underestimate your costs. Reviewers can and will recommend cutting your budget if they think your expenses are unwarranted, but they are unlikely to give you more funding if your budget was too low. You should round dollar amounts, but do not round to more than tens. If you round any higher, it will appear that you have not thoroughly researched your project.

When you plan your budget, allow for contingencies such as emergencies or increases in the cost of living. If you plan to purchase equipment, contact the distributor and inquire about the equipment's cost. In some instances, government grant makers may require you to surrender the equipment to them at the close of the grant.

As you read the budget's directions, realize that some donors do not want to see every item you purchase—for example, the 250 ink pens, 150 highlighters, and 175 pencils. These donors prefer that you indicate the supply cost, and then break the list into categories. However, other donors want to see everything. Either way, follow the donor's instructions.

In some instances, the grant proposal guidelines allow you to annotate your budget with footnotes. Footnotes are short comments that explain items in your budget by adding more details or by defining terms and meanings. However, only include footnotes when absolutely essential and useful.

Before you present your budget, check and recheck your math. Many people accidentally submit inaccurate numbers because they forgot to recalculate the budget amid the flurry of gathering and revising information. Once the budget is written, examine it line by line and then have someone else check it. Finally, review the budget a third time. Should you later realize you submitted a grant application with an error, send the funder the corrected page with a cover letter that explains your mistake.

Finally, you need to prepare a budget justification. This document explains why your project needs funding for the time you requested. You should inform the reviewers thoroughly (there is usually no page limit for this section), but do not overwhelm them.

Below is an example of a budget narrative:

Budget Narrative Example

- Personnel—List all of the personnel who will work on your project, their pay rate, and the percentage of time they work on the project.
- Fringe Benefits—Fringe benefits are added to salaries to cover pensions, unemployment, retirement, workers compensation, and other payroll costs.
- Travel—All travel costs should be listed. If you do not know how many conferences you will attend and/or the cost, a researched estimate will suffice. Travel expenses include airfare, mileage, daily expenses, registration, and other items.
- Consultants—All consultants should be listed, but if you do not know their exact cost, you can list a researched estimate.
- Equipment—Almost every funder has policies concerning permanent equipment, so read these guidelines. Funders want to know where you intend to purchase your equipment and what brands you plan to buy.

- Other—This section includes all other needed line items, such as telephone chargers, postage, printing, promotional material, and other items.
  Total of direct costs
  Total of indirect costs
  Grand total

While preparing a grant proposal's budget is not difficult, it can be tedious. However, if you provide the information that the donor requested, in the style indicated, you should have no problem completing a comprehensive and thoughtful proposal. Overall, writing the grant budget is as simple as filling in the blanks and adding—just like counting calories.

~~~

Maricia D. C. Johns is a published journalist and poet, editor, motivational speaker, and educator. She is a columnist for The Fort Worth Black News. Her editing credentials include works by Andre Johnson, Yolonda White, Tameka Lancaster and others. She is the owner of johnswriteme, a writing/speaking bureau. She has spoken at many different venues including Jarvis Christian College, Black Retired Educators Association, East Texas Writers Guild and many more.
~~~

Chapter 11

Approaching Secular Funders

By Joy Skjegstad

This is an excerpt of a chapter from Winning Grants to Strengthen Your Ministry, a book published originally by the Alban Institute in 2007. Used by permission.

> "We want to expand our housing ministry, but we're nervous about approaching foundation and corporate funders. We're concerned they would expect us to remove the faith component of our program."
>
> "I don't understand why so many foundations have trouble with the faith thing. What's the big deal whether we spend the money on praying with people or providing them with job training? It's all the same thing."
>
> "We know there's grant funding out there somewhere for the day care center at our church. What we do helps so many children that I know we'll have no trouble getting funding."

The need for nonprofit staff and boards to understand how to approach secular funders is one of the reasons I wanted to write this chapter. I encounter so many ministry groups that operate with inaccurate assumptions about how and why secular funders make grants, particularly to faith-based organizations. The quotes above are based on statements that people in ministry have made to me in over 20 years of professional fundraising. Some faith-based groups assume that grant funding for their ministries is out of the question. This isn't necessarily true. Some faith-based groups assume that getting grant funding for their ministry will be no problem at all. This isn't necessarily true, either.

What Are Secular Funders?

I broadly define "secular funders" as foundations or corporations that are <u>not</u> using their funding to achieve religious or spiritual goals. Frequently, these funders will have a sentence like this in their funding guidelines: "We will not fund religious organizations for religious purposes."

Among secular funders there are varying degrees of receptiveness to faith-based organizations. Funders are human beings who have their own perceptions of churches, faith, and spiritual matters. So you'll need to use your intuition to discern how open a particular funder is to partnering with faith-based organizations.

Just How Faith-Based Are You?

Understanding what faith-based means within your own organization is perhaps the best way you can prepare to approach secular funders. There have been many positive outcomes to the increased visibility of faith-based organizations in recent years, including the creation of new opportunities for funding and partnerships. One of the challenges, however, is the overuse of the phrase "faith-based." There appears to be no common thinking on what the term "faith-based" means. When I say "faith-based," I mean programs connected to congregations, but that don't necessarily have evangelistic content or goals. Someone else, however, may assume "faith-based" means that there is always an explicit religious component focused on converting participants. It's a loaded term, and in order to partner with secular funders, we need to define in very specific terms what "faith-based" means to us in our own organizations.

One way to assess how faith-based you are is to look at the spiritual content of your programs. I list some key questions to ask about this below. Another way is to look at how faith plays a role in the organizational aspects of your ministry such as funding, mission, and the selection of board members. Thinking through these issues will help prepare you to have conversations with secular funders. In the course of that conversation, you could expect to be asked the following kinds of questions:

- What are the spiritual components of your program? Prayer, Bible study, discipleship activities, church attendance?
- Is the spiritual component of your program optional or required for participants?
- Is the spiritual component of your program critical to its success?
- Are participants expected to participate in a particular church congregation in order to be a part of the program?
- Are staff members, board members, and volunteers expected to share the same faith commitment?

Sorting through the answers to these questions isn't always easy. For many of us, faith has become so key to the work that we do and so much a part of the way we live that it is difficult to separate it out from all the "other stuff." It seems artificial to make the separation at all. This is difficult work, but I encourage you to at least to try to think about the spiritual component as separate before you approach a secular funder.

Some Advice before You Approach a Secular Funder

These next sections offer specific advice on how you can approach secular funders. Take a step back first and consider this advice before you move into a conversation with a secular funder.

- Decide whether this particular funder is a fit for your program and organization. Sometimes you have to say "no." You may research a secular funder and decide that their terms just won't work for your ministry. If your program has a spiritual component that is imbedded into it, secular funding is probably not an option. Or you may find that particular secular funders are uncomfortable with informal spiritual content, or a connection to a particular church congregation, or the requirement that all of the board members express a Christian faith.

  Often you can determine whether there is a fit between the program and the funder by reading the funder's guidelines and annual report, or by having a phone conversation with them. Sometimes, however, the lack of fit won't come out until after you've submitted a proposal and have subsequent conversations. Whenever it becomes apparent that the funder wants something very different from what you do, you should end the process.
- Never hide your faith. Don't try to act like you're not faith-based if you are. *All of my advice in this chapter focuses on various ways to identify what it*

means for your organization to be faith-based and then how to talk about it. Be honest with funders about how faith figures in for your group. If you are connected to a particular church or denomination, say that. If most of your volunteers come from local faith communities, say that too. And, of course, if the spiritual component is an integral part of your programming that cannot be separated out, you have to communicate that to the funder, or you risk entering into a dishonest funding relationship.

- Never ask the funder for permission to conduct spiritual activities. Funders aren't setting the agenda for your organization, you are. So it is dangerous to put any funder in a "permission-giving" role. Don't ever approach a funder and ask questions like this: "Would it be all right for us to do Bible Study?" or "If we pray with folks would that be a problem?"

  Put yourself in the driver's seat on this issue, and using the tools on the previous pages, decide first what you mean when you say your organization is faith-based. This will help you identify how important the faith and spiritual components are to you and whether they can in any way be separated out from the rest of your program. Once you have done that work, you are prepared to talk to a secular funder.

- Anticipate objections about the faith component and respond to them up front. If you know you are approaching a funder who has concerns about your faith aspect, respond to their potential concerns right in the body of the grant. Be truthful, of course, but provide as many reassurances as you can. For example, many funders have concerns that faith-based organizations will only provide services to people from their particular church or of their particular faith. If that's not the case for you, include language like this in your proposal: "Our nonprofit organization was founded by Christians, but it serves a broad range of community members who subscribe to a wide range of religious beliefs."

- It is often appropriate to talk with funders about your own motivations for being involved in the ministry. Reflections on your own faith journey and how you got involved with your ministry organization can fit very easily into a conversation with a funder. Such discussion can be a great way for you to share your own witness and may bolster your funding request as you talk about the strength of your faith and how it has led you forward. I think too often we think we can't be ourselves around funders. This simply isn't true. As people of faith, we shouldn't try to hide our faith or leave it out of the picture just because we are asking for money. One caution about this: I wouldn't let your description of your faith journey be the main focus of the conversation. After all, the funder is there to take a look at your programs and decide whether they want to fund them.

Strategies for Approaching Secular Funders

I've identified four strategies that could work as you approach secular funders. Keep in mind that one strategy won't fit all funders. Each corporation and foundation is unique, and you should read each funder's guidelines carefully before choosing the strategy that you think would be most effective.

Strategy 1: Describe your ministry the way you see it and don't change a thing.

Sometimes faith-based groups feel called to describe themselves in their own language, leaving in all of the spiritual wording and content and taking their chances with the funders' response. This option is more about the language being used than anything else. I've found that people in ministry frequently have a particular way of talking. They use terms such as "new life in Christ" and "equipping the body of Christ." The value of this strategy is that you are as authentic as you can be when describing the work you do and you don't worry about what the funder wants to hear. The disadvantage, of course, is that you may alienate funders who are concerned about their money going to the spiritual aspects of programs, also funders who don't understand or who are confused by spiritual language.

Strategy 2: Exclude the spiritual aspect from the proposal entirely.

Another option to consider is to exclude the spiritual aspect from the proposal entirely. This only works if the spiritual aspect is minimal or if you feel you can clearly separate it out from the rest of your program. Otherwise, you risk being dishonest with the funder, which may result in a rejection of your grant and damage to your reputation in the funding community. Keep in mind that funders do talk with each other, so your dishonesty with one may affect your ability to get grants from other funders as well.

Some scenarios where it might work to leave the spiritual aspect out of the proposal entirely might include these:

- Your transitional housing program invites participants to an optional weekly Bible study sponsored by another organization. It's made clear to participants that they are not required to attend.
- Your arts center sponsors an exhibit of art with spiritual themes that is open to the entire community.

- Your youth center teaches a curriculum to kids based on Biblical concepts, but Bible passages themselves are not a part of the teaching. Youth consider how to be kind and honest, respect their parents, and encourage each other.
- Of course, if your organization is a church congregation, funders may still ask you about the spiritual component of your programs, even if it isn't mentioned in your proposal. Funders may assume that the congregational connection automatically means faith content. You could anticipate these questions by addressing the issue directly in your proposal, describing the nature of the relationship with the congregation and how faith figures into program content.

<u>Strategy 3:</u> Find other funding for the spiritual aspect of the program.

Separating out the spiritual aspect of your program and seeking other funding for it is another strategy that can help attract secular funding. Under this strategy, the spiritual component of your program is optional for participants and is completely funded by other sources, perhaps churches or individual donors. This approach assures a foundation or corporation that their funding will not be used for activities like Bible study or discipleship groups.

I would recommend that you still include the spiritual aspect of the program in the narrative of your proposal, in the interest of being totally honest with the funder. However, you can describe it briefly. Also, use terms that will be understood by the funder. (For example, leave out the heavy-duty theological language. See Strategy 4.)

In the budget for your proposal, you can still show the cost of the spiritual component, just clearly separate the costs and funding for it, showing it is distinct from the other components of the program. Be sure to include all costs of the spiritual component, including staff time devoted to it (and a corresponding portion of benefits), supplies, use of space, transportation, and a portion of your administrative expenses and overhead as well.

Strategy 4: Leave the spiritual aspect in the proposal, but describe it differently.

This strategy involves describing the spiritual or faith component of your program in terms that would be understood by and not threaten secular funders. *This is a change in language, not program content.*

As Christians, we can have the tendency to lapse into "church-speak," describing everything in Biblical or theological terms. This could be a hindrance to you as you seek funding from secular funders. First, you may give the impression that one of the primary objectives of your work is evangelistic, even when that is not the case. Second, you may confuse or threaten foundation staff members who don't have a church or theological background.

This strategy is based on the idea that there are different ways to talk about most everything, and changing your language can help open doors to conversations and potential funding. I have frequently used this strategy, and I always think about the apostle Paul in Athens when I do. Paul told the same story everywhere he went but altered his language to fit the context and the audience.

If you'd like to use this strategy, get someone outside of your ministry group to read your proposal and point out the places where you use faith language. Often it can be helpful to find someone who is not a Christian or who has some distance from the ministry world. Their perspective will be different from the one you get inside your ministry group. Then you can find a different way to describe the same thing.

Here are some examples of how you might use different language to describe your faith-based program:

Remove language like this	Replace it with this language
• Bible Study	• Spiritual Development
• Prayer	• Character building activities
• Proclaiming the Gospel	• (Avoid evangelism language)
• Equipping the body of Christ	• Recruiting and training volunteers
• Pastoral counseling	• Counseling and support groups
• Christ-centered programs	• Church-sponsored programs
• Showing the love of Christ	• Acting out our faith

No Compromise

The ultimate goal of ministry fundraising is to secure funding for your organization without compromising your mission and values. The tools and information in this chapter are provided with that goal in mind, not to encourage you to bend your organization or its programs to fit the mold of secular funders. You may decide after reading this chapter that secular funders are not a good fit for your ministry. That's a positive outcome since it helps you focus your efforts on funders that are the best fit for your group. Or reading this chapter may lead you to decide that you'd like to try to develop partnerships with secular funders. The very process of trying to form these partnerships can lead to positive outcomes as well, forcing examination of values and serving to clarify how faith is incorporated into the organization.

~~~

Joy Skjegstad is a national speaker and consultant on nonprofit management and ministry development. She has more than 20 years of experience starting and growing nonprofit organizations, with a special focus on faith-based groups and youth and community development. She has served as the Executive Director of the Park Avenue Foundation at Park Avenue United Methodist Church and is the founder of the Institute for Ministry Leaders, a university-based training program that builds the management capacity of churches and other ministry organizations.
~~~

Chapter 12

Applying for Federal Faith-Based Grants

By Hal Merz

For many years, the relationship between governmental agencies and faith groups was difficult, to say the least. Church-run organizations that received government grants were asked to remove crucifixes, religious art, and other expressions of faith from their offices or places where clients received services. Many faith groups found these restrictions burdensome.

In the 1980s, Dr. John DiUlio, a researcher at the University of Pennsylvania, began to write and speak extensively about social services provided by faith-based groups. He advocated for government partnerships with the faith-based sector. This beginning influenced several Presidential administrations, and resulted in the creation of the Office of Community and Faith-Based Programs during George W. Bush's presidency.

During the following decade, more than 30 states followed suite, establishing similar offices at the state level to encourage partnerships. This movement has enjoyed considerable bi-partisan support and there is good reason to believe it will continue.

Broadly speaking, the government will not fund programs for activities directly using specific religious teaching, or pay for salaries of religious workers or facilities used for religious worship. While some Christians find this policy troublesome, they should realize that it also prevents cultic or non-Christian religions from receiving financial support to promote their doctrines.

Government grants work best with faith-based groups that provide social or educational services to the general public. Food pantries, housing, job and economic development projects, afterschool programs, and preventative health and fitness programs are some examples. Christian colleges and universities can also receive government grants for purposes other than religion classes or majors that prepare religious workers.

Currently only a small fraction of the federal budget is targeted toward the activities of faith groups. The main emphasis is to increase access by creating policies that assure faith-based groups receive a fair and equitable treatment when grants are awarded. Recent studies suggest that the percentage of faith-based grant recipients has increased because of these policies.

It is often challenging to obtain a federal grant. Some of the popular federal programs have "success rates" of less than 10 percent. Generally speaking, if a given federal grant provides more than $250,000, and many types of organizations are eligible for it, there is strong competition. Smaller and more specialized grant competitions are less difficult, but in most cases, the success rate is no more than 20-30 percent.

Many of the federal grant proposals prepared by faith-based groups (and other types of small nonprofits with limited grant experience) are low quality. Most federal programs score grant proposals on a scale that has 1-100 points. It is not uncommon for a group of a dozen proposals to include several that score 10 points or less. To be competitive in most federal grant programs, a proposal should score 85 points or higher.

When the federal government reviews and scores proposals, it relies heavily on peer reviewers (groups of three or more people who are experts in their fields). In the past, these review panels flew to Washington and discussed the proposals in a series of meetings. Now, many of the reviews are conducted through online scoring and telephone conference calls.

Because the pay for reviewing proposals is moderate and the schedule is very demanding, the government has difficulty assuring every panel member is an expert in the specific area of the grant program being reviewed. Therefore, it is common for people from similar fields to be reviewers along with some panelists that are specific experts. For example, because of my education field background, I was asked to serve as reviewer for the Native American Vocational Education program. I have absolutely no familiarity with Native American populations or how their culture integrates with educational programs.

What are the implications of this for grant writers? Peer reviewers who are not experts rely legalistically on the published grant criteria. *You must explicitly describe how your proposal meets each and every point of the criteria*, even things that would be obvious to an expert in your field. This is difficult to do because stating the obvious feels condescending. However, I have never heard a grant proposal criticized for being overly detailed. On the contrary, I have seen many proposals criticized for lacking details, even if these details are obvious to the true expert.

Grant review panels are supervised either by federal program staff or by individuals who are experienced peer reviewers. In either case, they keep panelists on their toes and help them work toward consensus in scoring the proposals. Most agencies permit some variation in scores among reviewers, so a given proposal might receive scores of 77, 83 and 86 points from the three panelists. Then, the reviewers' scores are averaged (in this case, the average would be 82 points).

The federal staff may carefully check the work of panels that rate proposals either very high (e.g. over 90 points) or very low (less than 20 points), to assure that there are no clear biases in the reviewers' comments or places where they have misread the proposal. In some cases, organizations receive bonus points to break ties. For example, in 2005-2006, some programs awarded two bonus points to proposals from states and counties eligible for disaster aid due to Hurricane Katrina.

The program staff also verifies the applicant is an eligible recipient. For some large grants, the program staff may conduct field visits with applicant organizations to ensure that appropriate personnel and organizational safeguards are in place before making the grant.

After this evaluation process, the federal staff reviews the list of highly rated proposals so that the total dollar amount requested by these organizations can be met with the grant program budget. Lists of winning proposals are often shared with congressional staff before being released to the public. Winners receive written communication and may receive phone calls from program officers. Organizations that did not receive awards can request a copy of the panel reviewers' comments. Some agencies automatically send these comments to all applicants. Carefully read all comments because many give valuable advice about how to be successful in future grant competitions.

There are several important differences between federal grant proposals and proposals submitted to private foundations and corporations:

- Federal proposals are generally longer than private sector proposals because the government has professional staff with the time to read lengthier material, and because you must address program criteria, rules, and regulations in detail.
- Federal proposals are increasingly submitted online through the Grants.gov system, whereas many private foundations still prefer to receive material in the mail.
- Federal proposals are more likely to require matching funds in cash or in-kind services. This makes the budget section of federal proposals much more complex than typical foundation proposal budgets.
- Federal proposals place an even higher emphasis on program evaluation than private grants. In some cases, you may need to subcontract a professional who specializes in program evaluation in order to meet the grant requirements.
- Personal relationships and connections with program officers have less of a role in federal grants than in private sector grant writing.
- There is more technical jargon in federal grant applications than there is in private sector philanthropy. Federal grant announcements can be as long as 50 pages!

There are several things your organization should do to receive federal grants. The following section lays out a twelve-step program to assist your organization with this process:

1. Research your eligibility for federal grants that match your mission. Go to the website www.cfda.gov, which is the Catalog of Federal Domestic Assistance (CFDA). This is the government's catalog of the assistance that it provides to various types of organizations as well as to the general public. Search by keyword under the "Find Programs" link. For example, if you use the keyword "youth," you may find information like the sample shown below, which is an ex-offender program:

17.270 Reintegration of Ex-Offenders[28]

FEDERAL AGENCY: EMPLOYMENT AND TRAINING ADMINISTRATION, DEPARTMENT OF LABOR

AUTHORIZATION:
Workforce Investment Act of 1998, Title I, Subtitle D, Section 171, Public Law 105-220.

OBJECTIVES:
This program includes both Prisoner Reentry Initiative (PRI) grants to serve adult returning offenders and Youthful Offender grants aimed at youth involved or at risk of involvement in crime and violence. The objectives of the PRI grants include increasing the employment rate, employment retention rate, and earnings of released prisoners, and decreasing their recidivism. The objectives of the Youthful Offender grants include preventing in-school youth from dropping out of school, increasing the employment rate of out-of-school youth, increasing the reading and math skills of youth, reducing the involvement of youth in crime and violence, and reducing the recidivism rate of youth.

TYPES OF ASSISTANCE: Project Grants

USES AND USE RESTRICTIONS:

Services under the PRI grants include assistance in finding employment, mentoring, job training, remedial education, and other comprehensive transitional services. Services under the Youthful Offender grants include a wide array of educational, employment, mentoring, case management, and violence reduction efforts.

Applicant Eligibility:

Eligible applicants for PRI grants are faith-based and community organizations (FBCOs) that are located in, or have a staff presence in, the urban community being served. Eligible applicants for Youthful Offenders vary depending on the solicitation, but have included community-based organizations, school districts, and juvenile justice agencies.

Beneficiary Eligibility:

PRI grants serve individuals, 18 years old and older, who have been convicted as an adult and have been imprisoned for violating a state or federal law, and who have never committed a sex-related offense. Depending on the solicitation, enrollment may be limited based on whether the presenting offense was violent or whether the individual has previously committed a violent crime.

The entry above tells us that the program for Reintegration of Ex-Offenders is operated by the U.S. Department of Labor. Its authorization, or legal basis, comes from the Workforce Investment Act of 1998. Under types of assistance, the words "project grants" show that an organization can obtain funding to run projects. This is very important. If the words were "formula grant," the funds are pre-determined on a headcount basis, and there may be fewer opportunities for local nonprofits to start new programs.

Under applicant eligibility, faith-based and community organizations in urban areas are eligible, as are school districts and juvenile justice agencies. Under beneficiary eligibility, the people served are those over 18 who were tried and convicted as adults for criminal offenses other than sexual crimes.

2. Register your organization in the Grants.gov system. If you find one or more federal grants in the CFDA database that matches your mission, go to www.grants.gov. Register your organization as one that can apply online for federal grants. More than 95% of the federal grant processes require this online submission.

The registration process can be difficult to understand, and often takes more than one month to complete. You must go to several different websites to enter information. Your organization may need guidance from a nonprofit with previous experience to guide you through all the requirements.

Use the Grants.gov system to sign up to receive electronic notices when the grant programs you are interested in are about to be announced. For example, if you are interested in ex-offender programs, you could sign up to receive a notice whenever the program number 17.270, Reintegration of Ex-Offenders, looks for new grantees.

3. Contact the federal program officers. Learn about existing grant programs they have funded that are operating in your community and state. Use the phone numbers provided in the CFDA or Grants.gov listings. Ask if samples of previously-funded grant proposals can be sent to you.

Also, it is very important to ask federal staff to send you the program regulations and an example of the last RFP (request for proposals) or grant announcement for the particular program of interest. This will help prepare you to write the grant. There are some changes in RFPs from year to year, but much of the material remains the same unless there are major new regulations affecting that federal program.

4. Network with organizations that have received the grants. Collaboration is very important. By doing this, you can look for future partnership opportunities. You may also learn helpful hints about upcoming grants.

5. Attend workshops or briefings sponsored by the federal agency. These technical assistance workshops are often provided just before the formal grant announcement. The locations may include cities in your region as well as in Washington, D.C.

6. Begin developing your grant proposal before the official announcement appears in Grants.gov. Often there is as little as 30 days' warning before the due date by the time a grant is officially announced. That is almost never enough time to write a quality grant proposal. You should be working three to twelve months ahead.

7. Study the official announcement carefully. Compare it with the previous RFP to find any features or requirements that are new this time. Assign more than one person to read the announcement so they can compare notes.

8. Organize the proposal according to the announcement or by the grant evaluation criteria provided. If the announcement gives you a specific order in which to arrange the sections of your grant proposal, it is VERY important to follow

these instructions carefully. However, if there is no guidance, organize your proposal by the grant evaluation criteria in the order they are given: one section for each criterion that receives scoring points. This helps your grant reviewer and shows that you are well-organized.

9. Have another pair of eyes read the rough draft of your proposal. Someone outside the grant writing team should do this. For a small fee, you can hire a grant consultant to provide this review service.

10. Submit early to Grants.gov. Electronic grant systems have traffic jams on the due date, so try to submit the grant several days before the final day.

11. Ask for the official grant reviewer feedback. Whether you receive a grant or not, request the official feedback from the grant review process.

12. Study the reviewers' comments. Use the constructive criticism to begin planning your next grant proposal. Losing a grant is not the end but the start of the next opportunity!

~~~

Hal Merz is the President of a grants consulting firm, Paraclete Funding Resources, LLC. Hal has helped organizations write proposals scoring a perfect 100 points with three major federal grant programs. He also has a $21 million grants development track record. He has frequently been a grant reviewer and supervisor of grant reviews for federal agencies, including the Compassion Capital program.
~~~

Chapter 13

Writing the Federal Faith-Based Grant Proposal

By Cheryl Kester

The previous chapter addresses information that faith-based organizations should understand when applying for federal grants. This chapter focuses on completing a federal application.

Deciding Whether to Apply

Writing a federal grant proposal can be intimidating because there are many rules and regulations. Acronyms. "Allowable" and "unallowable" costs. Matching funds. Strange forms like 424A and 424B. And of course, the Grants.gov system used to submit applications.

You should consider several factors before competing for federal funds, including whether your organization can abide by the rules about religion that come with federal grant funds. Usually, you are allowed to follow your existing hiring practices and do not have to remove religious symbols from your walls or change your name.

However, you cannot conduct religious activities at the same time and in the same place as federally-funded grant activities. For example, you cannot combine Bible study with your anti-gang youth program if a federal grant is paying for the program. This is known as the "separate in time and place" concept. Otherwise, there is no reason why a faith-based organization cannot successfully compete for federal funding

Once you understand these factors and decide to apply, the basics of preparing quality grant proposals remains the same no matter who you are: Follow the guidelines. Use the funder's language. Meet the funder's priorities. Present clear, detailed writing. Allow no room for misunderstandings by your readers.

It Must be A+

Other than the sheer size of the application, federal grant applications are different from foundation applications because every point counts. Federal applications are usually scored by reviewers who follow a rubric, a set of points assigned to each section.

Most federal grants are highly competitive—I have written and reviewed proposals during competitions where only applications scoring 98.6 points or more out of 100 even made it to the finalists' list.

You cannot afford to write an application that risks losing a single point.

Take the Team Approach

One way to ensure your application meets all of the requirements and that you don't need a signature from the Chairman of the Board who left for vacation two days before the grant is due, is to create a team of people to prepare the application.

These are the kinds of people you should have on your team:

- *The Visionary* has the dream and sees how your project will change the world. This person understands the big picture.
- The *Warrior* has daily experience in making the vision reality. This person balances the visionary with practical knowledge: for example, this person knows how long it takes to receive visas to do relief work in Somalia or how many tons of food your soup kitchen needs to feed 75 people a week.
- The *Numbers* person loves creating and revising budgets.
- The *Scavenger* locates data, statistics, quotations, footnotes, and other details to put in the proposal.
- The *Nit-Picker Extraordinaire* carefully proofs your proposal to ensure every detail is correct. If you changed the number of people to be served in Year 3, the nit-picker makes sure this number is the same in the work plan, the budget, the budget narrative, and everywhere else.
- The *Organizer/Writer* pulls all of these components together into an orderly, easy-to-follow manner that meets all of the guidelines' requirements.
- The *Outside Reader* is a trusted colleague who is not involved in the grant proposal construction. Once you are ready to submit your proposal, this person reads your proposal and looks for things you might have missed or that do not make sense.

Following the Guidelines

Most federal agencies give grant applicants very detailed instructions for completing a proposal. These Requests for Proposals (RFPs) can reach 45 to 80 pages.

While this seems like an overabundance of information, these detailed instructions are a roadmap to success if followed carefully. When competing for federal grants every point counts, and if the guidance tells you how those points are allocated, then you know how to respond.

Here is an excerpt from the guidance for one federal program for rural health care services[29]:

> *The target population and its unmet health needs must be described and documented in this section [...] Describe the entire population of the service area and its demographics in relation to the population to be served. Local data, which is particularly important if available, should be used to document the unmet health needs in the target population. This data should be compared to State and national data. Also, use factors that are relevant to the project, such as specific health status indicators, age, etc.*

A successful proposal would respond to every idea expressed in the above paragraph. Label each idea clearly and arrange them in the order given in the guidance sheet.

Outlining the Grant Guidance

After the guidance for this year's competition is released, read the RFP several times with a highlighter in hand. Once you understand the big picture, look for everything the guidance wants included in the project narrative, and then pull these items into one list.

Use your newly created list as an outline. Later, you will insert relevant content, data, and statistics into the appropriate sections. For example, the above sample paragraph would probably be outlined as:

A. Describe the target population
   a. demographics
   b. population to be served
B. Describe this population's unmet health needs
   a. document the needs (especially local data)
   b. compare local data to state/national data
   c. use factors relevant to project

The outline is a quick overview that allows everyone on your proposal team to see what information is needed. Since finding data and statistics can be a lengthy process, the scavenger can work on data while you finalize the program design or tweak the budget.

Attachments Take Time

You have a long narrative to write. You must design a multi-year plan and balance your budget. While these are critical to your application's success, do not forget that most federal applications also have several extra forms. Certifications and assurances must be signed, letters from partners or supporters are needed, and sometimes, several attachments with additional information are requested.

At the same time you create the narrative outline, make a checklist for the total application package. The very first time your organization applies for a federal grant, you will probably need to send all of the certifications, assurances, lobbying disclosures, and regulations to an attorney who can review them and ensure that you are in compliance with the laws governing the program. Also, someone should request letters of support from your congressional delegation or a Memoranda of Understanding from all of your partners. Finally, someone from your organization must register your ministry with Grants.gov, a process that can take weeks. A failed Grants.gov registration guarantees your application will never reach the review panel.

Don't Neglect the Budget

Do not fall into the temptation of waiting until the end to write your project budget. It is essential to develop your budget when you develop your basic project ideas. It is pointless to spend hours or even days getting all of the program details designed perfectly for a project that is over budget or proposes to use grant funds for unallowable costs.

The RFP usually states in general terms what the grant funds may or may not be used for in that particular program. Second, any budget item must be reasonable, necessary and allowable. You make an argument for why items are reasonable and necessary in your budget narrative. You determine whether a cost is allowable by following a government publication called OMB Circular A-122, "Cost Principles for Non-Profit Organizations." This document, available for free online, offers very specific guidance regarding what grant funds may or may not be spent on. Every federal grant applicant is expected to be familiar with this list of allowable versus unallowable costs.

If you submit an application for a multi-year project, make sure to create an extremely detailed budget for each year of the project, even if you are only required to submit the budget for Year 1 with your application. This ensures you can continue to successfully offer your program in subsequent years.

Once the budget is complete, write the budget narrative (the document that accompanies the budget). In this document, you explain every line item in your budget, how you arrived at the cost (show your math if possible), and why that item or service is critical to your program's success. You are selling your budget plan to the reader, who will naturally be skeptical.

Finally, you must understand direct and indirect costs. If your organization is new to federal grants, you will probably not need to negotiate an indirect cost rate. However, once you have several federal grants awarded simultaneously, you and your accountant should explore the possible benefits of an indirect cost rate. Indirect costs are expenses that cannot be readily tied to your particular program but are still necessary for general operations. However, until you have a negotiated rate, most agencies do not allow you to request indirect costs. You can only request direct costs (costs tied directly to operating the proposed project such as salaries for project staff, supplies needed to teach the classes, etc).

Reaching Those Scoring Your Proposal

Once the outline is done and the other assignments made, it's time to start writing. The writer's job is to fill in the proposal's outline blanks. All of them. Thoroughly. Use language that is easy to understand. Leave adequate white space and include clear headers so reviewers can find each key point. Insert tables, charts, graphics, and maps when appropriate.

For example, when you write the section about need, you may be responding to a similar paragraph[30]:

> *The target population and its unmet health needs must be described and documented in this section [...] Describe the entire population of the service area and its demographics in relation to the population to be served. Local data, which is particularly*

important if available, should be used to document the unmet health needs in the target population. This data should be compared to state and national data. Also, use factors that are relevant to the project, such as specific health status indicators, age, etc.

You should clearly mark each section by providing a header using the RFP's own language: "The target population is…" Later, you will begin another sentence with, "The target population's unmet health needs include..." Do not be concerned that this seems elementary or that you will offend your readers. They welcome this kind of clarity because it makes their job easier.

Effective proposal writers always write for their audience. They appeal to their reader by adopting their audience's language, style, and tone. The writer's job is to make the reviewer's job as easy as possible. Reviewers are tired. They may be in a hurry. They may not understand who you are or why your organization would be a good investment for their tax dollars.

At the risk of stating the obvious, don't describe your organization as a ministry. If staff members are paid with grant funds, don't use titles like "Minister of Youth Outreach." Finally, never imply that grant funds will be used for religious activities.

While you should not write empty text just to take up space, you almost always need all of the space allowed to adequately respond to the guidance. If your narrative is several pages short of the maximum, review the minutiae of the guidelines to make sure you have not missed anything.

Meeting the Funder's Priorities with Your Program

If you request funds to provide marriage enrichment services, it is perfectly acceptable to discuss how strengthening marriages positively impacts communities, families, and children. However, it will be less effective, possibly bother some reviewers, and may even jeopardize your funding if you speak of these services as a ministry. Similarly, when you describe your community's need for marriage services, you must do so objectively—state statistics about failed marriages; don't quote Scriptural injunctions against divorce.

Remember, you are writing to an audience that may share your desire for strong marriages, but might not share your faith. Some reviewers and agency staff are uncomfortable with federal dollars going to religious organizations, so they may be searching for ways to award your proposal fewer points.

The best way to avoid this is to present your nonprofit as a capable, professional, experienced organization that effectively provides services to a particular population.

It's a Matter of Emphasis

I am not suggesting that you hide your religious identity. If your ministry's name is "Bringing God's Love to our Neighbors," then proudly state your name. Only, for the purpose of a federal grant proposal, refer to your ministry as an "organization." Emphasize the social and human services "Bringing God's Love" provides in your community, not its ministries. Never try to pull a "fast one" on reviewers, but be aware how Christian jargon sounds to outsiders.

Watch for words with religious overtones that are probably part of your everyday vocabulary, and then replace them with more neutral terms.

I have participated on federal grant review panels that scored proposals from organizations that tried to demonstrate their effectiveness by listing how many people had been saved and how many residents were now church members. Not surprisingly, these well-meaning organizations did not receive the grants they were seeking.

Conclusion

Yes, faith-based organizations can compete effectively for federal grants. If you decide that a federal grant is right for your organization and you attend to the basic rules outlined above, you can also be successful.

~~~

Cheryl Kester is a partner with Thomas-Forbes & Kester and a member of the American Association of Grant Professionals. She has written grants for federal faith based initiatives as well as private foundation grants. She frequently teaches on grant writing and grant review. She is a Certified Fundraising Executive (CFRE). Previously, she was the Director of Grants and Foundation Relations at John Brown University.
~~~

Chapter 14

Planned Giving Success for Small Nonprofits

By Bob Crew

If you are reading this chapter, you are at least curious about the potential for planned giving in your organization. Planned giving is either a way donors can leave money or assets to an organization after the individual's death, or an investment plan that allows the donor to receive benefits during his or her lifetime, with the remaining funds going to the organization after the donor's death. However, planned giving requires organizational resources, and since the results are typically not immediate, you must first develop support for this initiative within your organization. Do not take for granted that your executive director or board members understand the value of planned giving in your organization. Below are a few responses to the question, "Why should our organization launch a planned giving program?"

Why Launch Planned Giving?

- *Our best donors are aging.* Most organizations' best and most consistent donors are part of the builder generation (those born before 1945) and will pass away in the next 15 – 20 years. Demographic statistics tell us that this age group is passing away at the rate of 5,000 per day. If you do not have a planned giving program that captures the generosity of your faithful donors, their support will eventually come to an end.

- *We are fishing in a small pond.* Less than 10% of the average American holds net worth is in cash. The remaining 90% of wealth is in various forms such as residences, retirement plans, investment, real estate, private business interests, personal belongings, etc. Without a planned giving program, you are limited to "fishing" for support where the resources are limited.
- *We need to get in the game.* Donors are increasingly aware of the benefits of planned giving. Banks, financial institutions, insurance companies, and other ministries are marketing planned gifts, like charitable trusts and donor-advised funds, to your donors. There is a growing understanding of these strategies and tools, and your donors need to know that you are "in the game" so that they will come to you when they want to explore these ideas. Otherwise, they will look elsewhere for help.
- *Organizational stability.* One significant benefit to having a sustained and successful planned giving program is that endowment funds provide consistent funding independent of economic downturns, loss of donors, and government programs. What organization could not more effectively plan and execute its mission if it had more consistent and predictable sources of funding?
- *Stronger donor relationships.* Planned giving allows you to engage your donors in conversations about the

mission, vision, and future direction of your organization. As a result, donors become more devoted to your mission and tend to increase their annual giving in addition to making planned gifts.

- *An opportunity to serve your donors.* Planned giving focuses on the needs of your donor. When you enter the planned giving discussion with a donor, the focus is on them, not on your organization. You help donors solve personal, family, and business problems. The tools and strategies employed result in a double benefit for your donors: a problem or concern solved and the satisfaction of a gift to an organization they care deeply about. Now that's "win-win."

You will undoubtedly find more reasons specific to your organization for initiating a planned giving program. Remember to be well-grounded in the rationale behind planned giving. Make sure your organization is solidly behind this initiative because it is a long-term commitment that requires time, money, and organizational energy to be successful.

What Motivates Donors to Make Planned Gifts?

One of the most common mistakes made when launching a planned giving program is to incorrectly appeal to the donor's motivations. Since planned giving usually involves significant income tax benefits for donors (and who doesn't like to save on income taxes), organizations mistakenly think tax savings are the primary motivation for planned giving. However, study after study of donor motivation reports this is not true. Tax savings are just one reason why donors make planned gifts, but it is not a primary motivation. Depending on the study you choose to read, donor motivation generally falls in the following priority sequence:

- Belief in the mission and/or vision of the organization
- Relationship to organizational leadership
- Desire to help others
- Desire to make a difference
- Desire to leave a legacy
- Gratitude
- Obligation
- Income and estate tax benefits
- Recognition
- Simplification

Studies consistently show there is a big drop-off in motivational influence after the first two items listed above. Planned giving is very different than raising support for an annual budget, so do not make the mistake of emphasizing the tax benefits of planned giving. Focus on mission and vision. Take time to develop deep relationships with your donors and help them feel connected to your organization.

The tax benefits of planned giving are the same no matter what organization the donor elects to support. Therefore, you cannot distinguish yourself in the donor's heart with tax incentives. You must touch a donor's heart with your mission. Your best results will come when you link a donor to a cause, an ideal, or a mission.

Before You Launch

The foundation of your planned giving program is laid long before you send out your first mailing announcing your new initiative. You must have appropriate systems, procedures, policies, and staffing established before you launch. You must also obtain the technical expertise needed to execute your planned giving program.

Long-term Commitment. Your board and executive leadership must be willing to make a five year commitment to planned giving. Expecting a monetary return on this investment in the first three years leads to frustration. You may get lucky and close a significant noncash gift early on, but you should not count on that. Monetary benefits will begin to trickle in during years three through five. Subsequent years will produce benefits exponentially higher than traditional fundraising. Do not give up too soon. By launching planned giving, your organization is signaling that it is maturing and is here to stay. Killing the program after two years because you have not received immediate results sends the opposite message.

Policies and Procedures. Your planned giving policies and procedures should be in place before you launch your program. Don't wait until a donor wants to give you a piece of real estate to decide how your board will accept it. Well-designed policies save you from making bad decisions and long-term commitments that you cannot keep. Furthermore, donors take comfort in knowing there is already a plan in place for their gift. Since many planned gifts are received years after the commitment is made, your donor will look to your policies and procedures to ensure that their gift will be used and managed wisely.

Administrative Systems. Do not overlook a donor contact management system that is designed to track donor contacts and record planned gifts. This is much more than an accounting system to record cash gifts. You need a system that allows you to record all your donor contacts (mailings, personal visits, phone conversations, etc.), personal information (birthdays, anniversaries, names of children and grandchildren, professional advisors, etc.), and future gift commitments that do not appear in accounting software (bequests, remainder interests, etc.). Planned giving success is based on relationship development, so you should have systems to assist you with this important task.

Technical Expertise. This can be one of the most daunting challenges facing a small nonprofit that hopes to engage donors in planned giving. Since planned giving touches so many areas—legal issues, taxation, financial planning, inheritance planning, and estate planning—most small nonprofits do not have internal resources with expertise in all these fields. There are several ways to resolve this challenge:

1. *Partner with a community foundation.* Community foundations are great resources for small nonprofits and can provide many administrative functions, legal and tax resources, marketing ideas, and investment management expertise. By partnering with a community foundation, you can focus on your core strengths of donor identification and relationships. When a planned giving opportunity is identified, you can call the community foundation for technical, legal, tax, and transaction execution assistance. This is a classic situation of small (and some not so small) organizations sharing the burden of unique or expensive expertise to keep costs down and to maintain focus on core strengths.
2. *Develop professional networks.* Attorneys, accountants, and financial advisors all have a vested interest in the success of your planned giving program. Create a network of professional advisors that you can call when a planned giving opportunity arrives. Most are happy to assist you because they have an opportunity to gain a new client and to help you accomplish your mission.

The Accountability Trap. The sustainability of a planned giving program depends on accountability. Another common mistake made by small nonprofits is to add planned giving to the job description of existing staff members. The staff person's current responsibilities are already time sensitive, and there are deadlines. Inevitably and even unintentionally, the tyranny of the urgent pushes out the important, but not urgent, task of planned giving. This happens time and time again. Here is the solution: planned giving should be the sole responsibility of the person to whom it is assigned. It can be a volunteer, part-time staff person, or an outside consultant, but he or she should only be accountable for this task. This way, there is no conflict between the urgent and the important.

Marketing

Once you have made the case for planned giving and laid the foundation, you are ready to begin marketing. So, with all the tools and strategies available, where do you start? The two greatest indicators of a donor's propensity to make a planned gift are the frequency of giving and the longevity of giving. Don't be fooled into thinking that the size of gift is the best indicator of planned gift potential. Know your donor base and focus your relationships on longtime, frequent givers. That annual $250 donor who has given to you for 15 or 20 years could be a $100,000 planned gift.

Planned giving prospects need a reason and a place to give. When a donor writes a check for your organization's annual fund or building campaign, the gift's use and purpose are already known. However, with a planned gift commitment, the actual receipt of funds may be many years down the road. Donors still want to know what their gifts will support. You need to identify three to five "buckets" that donors can direct their planned gifts toward. Your buckets should be closely identified with your particular mission/vision and should be ministry related, such as scholarships, hunger relief, children and youth, etc. You can always include a bucket titled "Area of Greatest Need" to give your organization's future leadership the flexibility to direct funds as necessary.

What to Market

Bequests. 80% of all planned gifts are simple estate plan bequests from a last will and testament or revocable living trust. This should be your first area of emphasis because bequests appeal to everyone in your donor base no matter what their economic status. These gifts can be very significant in size. The largest known bequest to an operating charity (not a public or private foundation) was in excess of $1 billion. Make sure your literature and website contain instructions on how to leave your organization a bequest.

Charitable Gift Annuities. The second most prevalent form of planned gifts is the gift annuity, which was pioneered in the United States in the 1800s by the American Bible Society. Target your senior donors age 70+ for this gift tool that produces high guaranteed lifetime income to the donor with the residual coming to your charity. Partner with a community foundation or another charitable organization to handle the administrative details until your volume reaches a level that justifies handling these within your company.

Noncash Gifts. Real estate, personal property, stocks, mutual funds, life insurance policies, collections, business inventory, and private business interests are examples of gifts that can be given to your organization. These are direct gifts that result in an immediate infusion of funds for your charity. If you do not have the legal and technical expertise to work with these gifts, a community foundation is a very valuable resource.

Donor Advised Funds. This is an increasingly popular tool used to solve the donor's multiple objectives: capital gains avoidance, creation of a family foundation, and income tax liability management. Most community foundations provide the infrastructure for a donor-advised fund program that your organization can access as if it were your own program.

Structured Gifts. Charitable remainder trusts and charitable lead trusts fall into this category. These tools usually have some incentive for income or estate tax reduction and are often utilized by high net worth individuals.

How to Market Planned Gifts

The marketing tools for planned giving include print material, web, email, letters, and workshops. There are numerous sources for sample materials and vendors who provide print and electronic services for purchase. Remember, while seniors are increasingly using the Internet, their generation still likes to hold something tangible as they read. Whenever possible, include planned giving literature or highlight a planned giving concept in communication you are already sending to your donors. For example, include a brochure with quarterly or annual giving statements, or a letter from the executive director. Also, incorporate a planned giving message or emphasis in any donor event you host and in every face-to-face donor meeting. Sow planned giving seeds everywhere you have donor contact.

Most importantly, focus on your message. Here are rules to live by as you market planned gifts:

1. Market your organization, not planned gifts. Remember, a donor's decision to give is emotional/relational while the decision how to give is rational/logical. Don't emphasize the gift instrument; focus on your organization's mission and effectiveness.
2. Use testimonials. People like to read stories. Have your donors explain why they decided to support you and how incredible it made them feel. Others also want to feel good. Stories inspire us to action and appeal to our emotional/relational side.
3. Explain how planned giving solved problems or alleviated concerns. Show donors how they can solve their own challenges and do something good for others through your organization.

There are many good resources available for a small nonprofit interested in launching a planned giving program. Here are a few:

- *Planned Giving for Small Nonprofits*. Ronald R. Jordan, Katelyn L. Quynn
- *The Complete Guide to Planned Giving*. Debra Ashton
- *Planned Giving Today*. Mary Ann Liebert, Inc., publisher
- *Planned Giving Mentor*. Mary Ann Liebert, Inc., publisher

Many small nonprofits desire to initiate a planned giving program but struggle with implementation issues. However, this chapter's overview of the critical elements for success and pitfalls to avoid will aid you as you begin this new venture.

~~~

Bob Crew has worked in investment management, financial planning, and charitable giving since 1986. In 2002, Bob started Planned Stewardship, LLC as a fee-only consultant to charities to assist with the structure and execution of planned giving programs. Bob's clients include regional and national charities. Bob is a member of the CFA Institute, Financial Planning Association, Partnership for Philanthropic Planning, the Central Kansas Planned Giving Roundtable, and is a Qualified Kingdom Advisor.
~~~

Chapter 15

Creative Alternatives to Foundation Giving

By Debbie Farrar

As a twenty-year veteran in foundation and corporate fundraising, I've observed many changes in the foundation world. There are three major trends that affect ministries' abilities to approach foundations:

1. Diminishing assets
2. An increase in anonymous gifts through community foundation donor advised funds
3. Proactive foundations that no longer accept unsolicited proposals but instead seek out ministries that interest them.

These shifting circumstances compel ministries to think creatively and to look for alternatives to the standard process of grant seeking. Several years ago, I began to pray about my chosen career path, and I regularly asked God to show me what was changing and how I might change with it. As a trainer and consultant, it is my job to mentor ministries, and I needed to guide ministries for tomorrow's philanthropy—not today's. While the process was not easy and philanthropic giving continues to change, two new concepts are worth deliberation. This chapter looks at these two new concepts in philanthropy: Venture Philanthropy and Income-Producing Ministry.

Venture Philanthropy

Venture philanthropy is a combination of income-producing investment and philanthropic giving. It combines the best of investing and philanthropy to benefit the investor and the donor.

Traditional fundraising tactics, like capital campaigns, can be time and human resource intensive, taxing even the most savvy fundraising team and executive staff. It can also create donor fatigue in communities that have already seen many similar campaigns.

Venture philanthropy was first introduced in 2000-2001, but now it is emerging as an excellent alternative to the traditional capital campaign. Venture philanthropy can shorten the length of a capital campaign by 75 percent or more. It can decrease donor fatigue, generate income, and provide tax incentives and benefits for the donor and venture philanthropist over a seven year period. It will also benefit the nonprofit that is the recipient of the building and land. It can be financially beneficial for both the ministry and the donor.

The venture philanthropy concept is as follows:

- A small group of interested venture philanthropists (typically seven to 10 people) capable of collectively purchasing some land and a building form a limited liability company (LLC).
- The LLC is formed as agreed upon by the venture philanthropists, the nonprofit organization, and the LLC's tax attorneys and accountants.

- Two separate legal and binding agreements are drafted and agreed upon.
- Details of this agreement should be flexible enough to satisfy the interests of each venture philanthropist. Also, the ministry should include clauses in each contract that protect the ministry, mission integrity, and donor interests. Terminology in these agreements should state that the ministry's purposes will not substantively change or become less evangelical; this protects the ministry's mission and integrity.
- The LLC and the ministry sign a separate memorandum of agreement that outlines the contract to lease for a seven-year period followed by the outright donation of the said land and building to the ministry.
- The LLC purchases the land and constructs the building that will house the ministry.
- The LLC leases the land and building to the ministry for a specified period of time (typically seven years).
- The LLC depreciates the building over the seven year period as specified by the LLC's accountant and tax attorneys and as outlined by state and federal tax laws.
- During the seven-year lease while investors depreciate the building, the LLC collects lease from the ministry at fair market value.
- At the end of the agreed upon depreciation/lease period, the land and building are fully donated to the ministry, and the LLC receives another tax deduction for the building donation, minus depreciation, as governed by state and federal tax laws.
- The LLC receives a donation receipt for the current fair market value of the land and building at end of the seven-year lease agreement. While the

LLC may have invested $3,500,000 at the time the LLC was formed, its tax deduction is based on the fair market value of the property at the end of the seven-year period, conceivably in the $4 - $5 million range depending on the annual rate of real estate appreciation.

- By the end of the seven-year period, the ministry no longer has a mortgage or lease payment. This allows the ministry to annually place approximately $150,000 - $200,000 into direct ministry programs instead of applying it to overhead costs related to loan repayment or rent.

Now that the building and land have been provided, a capital campaign must only raise funds for computers, office equipment, and staff positions for the expanded program; this is probably only 20 percent of the original campaign budget. Donors are more likely to donate to the last 20 percent needed in a campaign when they feel the largest portion of the campaign is already fully funded.

Let's look at one of six hypothetical investors. One venture philanthropist invests $750,000 (one-sixth share) in a $4.5 million land and building project. The funds are invested in an LLC created for the sole purpose of building a facility for a ministry. For each of the seven years, the investor receives standard depreciation on his or her share of the building and collects a proportionate share of the fair market rent on the facility the LLC built. The ministry is the rent-paying tenant for these seven years.

At the end of seven years, the LLC deeds the land and building to the ministry as agreed upon in the second legal agreement. Then, the LLC receives a tax deduction, minus depreciation, based on the current fair market value of the facility. Standard appreciation is generally three to five percent annually. A building built for $4.5 million would be valued at approximately $5.92 million by the end of year seven. The combination of depreciation, rental income, and tax deduction returns all but approximately $190,000 to the venture philanthropist.

Multiply this by each of the six investors, and the LLC collectively deeds a $6 million dollar building to the ministry for a combined out-of-pocket expense of $1.14 million at the end of seven years. This is leveraged philanthropy!

Venture philanthropy is beneficial for both donors and ministries from tax, donor, investment, and ministry standpoints. It appeals to donors who like to gain the highest possible return on their gift and who want to see the long term impact of their gift. It also appeals to entrepreneurs who want to be philanthropic and involved in planning a deal that benefits the investor and the ministry.

While venture philanthropy is moderately new, increasingly more attorneys, accountants, Christian business people, and philanthropists are looking for creative ways to fund their favorite ministries, leverage their philanthropic giving, and stretch their investment dollars to their fullest capacity.

It takes time and careful planning to find a core group to invest in an LLC. A well-developed business plan, architectural drawings, and carefully designed informational packets distributed to the ministry's potential investors are critical to success.

Income-Producing Ministry

The self-sustaining model of fund development is a second alternative to traditional fundraising that ministries should consider. As traditional sources of funding decrease and the demand for those financial resources increase, ministries should look within their programs, projects, and mission to see if a program could be developed to generate income.

First, does your ministry have a creative idea that is needed by the community your ministry serves or a product that could be released nationally or internationally that would produce income for your operating budget? If so, put that idea to work. Foundations and individual donors, particularly the younger, more entrepreneurial donors of today's philanthropy, are intrigued by the possibility of investing in a program that sustains a ministry long-term.

Investing in such an income-producing program decreases the demand for ongoing program support and lessens the burden on your ministry's development team. Because foundations typically receive ten times as many proposals as they can fund, your proposal concept must attract the attention of the reader. Foundations don't want to sustain your ministry forever and this type of entrepreneurial thinking may stimulate a closer look at your proposal, and ultimately, a grant.

Donors are greatly interested in helping you build programs or projects that are self-sustaining and do not require repeated grants to fund ongoing ministry programs.

Conclusion

It is vital that Kingdom-minded ministries efficiently use the funds they receive and that they leverage those dollars to their maximum capacity.

It is said that it only takes 10 years for a nonprofit organization to become a well-established institution. However, in order to reach that place, your ministry must think creatively and look carefully at how and why you do what you do. You must be willing to change your perspective. Ultimately, you must prayerfully analyze your strengths and weaknesses and identify any barriers to growth.

Ministries cannot be complacent. You should avoid institutional thinking and diligently seek the mind of Christ. Honor and acknowledge Him and allow Him to show you the way. Take to heart Proverbs 3:5-6, "Trust in the Lord with all your heart and do not lean on your own understanding. In all your ways acknowledge Him, and He will make your paths straight."[31]

As tomorrow's donors look for creative and leveraged ways to support the Great Commission while being good stewards of the assets entrusted to them, ministries must also think creatively and tenaciously pursue careful stewardship of the funds they receive.

~~~

Debbie Farrar has extensive development experience, including work with Regents University, International Bible Society, and Dawn Ministries. Debbie has been a fund development trainer/consultant since 1998. She has worked with many faith-based and nonprofit organizations across the country including Josh McDowell Ministries, Awana International, Trans World Radio, Operation Mobilization, Christian and Missionary Alliance, and Cook Communications.
~~~

Chapter 16

Starting A Church Foundation

By William F. High

Introduction

Not long ago, I met with a pastor of a large Baptist church. He described how a member had passed away, and it had been his understanding that the church was to receive $500,000 from the estate. However, the church member had specifically prescribed that the gift was to go into the church foundation. Unfortunately, the church had never established a foundation, and consequently the gift was not made. As the pastor told me this story, he related two similar lost opportunities for his church.

As the generations from World War II and the Korean War have begun to pass away, there has been an increasing interest in establishing endowments or church foundations. This interest has particularly become heightened as the nearly 80 million Boomers are reaching retirement age. And like the pastor in the story above, the idea of establishing a church foundation is often essential to the basics of even receiving an estate gift.

This chapter will lay out some of the basics of starting a church foundation.

Purpose and Overview

The purpose of this chapter is to answer the basic questions behind having a church foundation. Those questions are the following:

1. What are the basics of biblical stewardship?
2. What is a church foundation?
3. How does it work?
4. Why is it important?
5. What are the pathways to growth for the church foundation?
6. What are the next steps in moving forward?

However, this chapter is not designed to cover everything related to church stewardship. There are many other topics that could be addressed, including sermons on stewardship, small group financial studies, seminars, children/youth, and capital campaigns.

On the other hand, it should be noted that the Church Foundation will best move forward if the pastor, staff and leadership board have all agreed that stewardship is a vital component of the church ministry.

Basics of Biblical Stewardship

We begin with the basics of biblical stewardship. We do so because, while many understand those basics, we find that many do not. In fact, we know that many churches avoid the topic of stewardship altogether. If they do not avoid it, then they tiptoe gently around it. A proper understanding of the basics of biblical stewardship allows us to confront the topic head on just as if we were dealing with any other subject—evangelism, discipleship, etc.

So what are the basics of biblical stewardship? We think that there are at least five issues that must be addressed. They might be summed up as follows:

1. It's all God's.
2. It's not mine.
3. This is not my home.
4. I will be held accountable.
5. There is reward and loss.

It's All God's.

God is the owner of everything. Ps. 24:1 says, "The earth is the Lord's, and ***all*** it contains; the world, and those who dwell in it." This principle of God's ownership is perhaps one of the most forgotten teachings in the church today. God owns everything—our houses, our land, our companies, our possessions, even our lives and the very seconds that we live.

This principle also cuts against the common teaching of the church—the tithe. Often the church teaches the tithe, or 10 percent, as the goal of giving. Consequently, we've had people who literally did not realize they could give more than 10 percent. To the contrary, God is the 100 percent owner of everything and could require any individual to give 100 percent.

It's Not Mine.

Because God is the owner of everything, it means that I own nothing. What then is my role with what God has given me—a steward. I'm a manager. God entrusts me with possessions, but my role is to manage them for His sake and His glory.

As in Matthew 25, and the parable of the talents, my role is to take the talents of the Master and invest them well so they return a "profit" for His sake. My management extends to everything—my use of time, my use of the talents and skills and abilities that He's given me, my use of financial resources (however much), my use of His Word, and my use and management of the relationships that He's put in my care.

This is not my home.

In Hebrews 11, the Hall of Fame of faith, the great mark of our faith heroes is that they recognized that this earth was not their home. Peter called us "aliens and exiles," (I Peter 2:11). David called us "sojourners and tenants," (I Chronicles 29:15). We are just passing through this life. As James says, our life on this earth is a vapor or a mist.

The mistake that we often make is that we treat our work on this planet as the goal. The great goal of American culture is to store up and accumulate for retirement so we can take it easy. The adage goes: "Make all you can, save all you can so you can sit on your can!"

Our ultimate home, however, is in heaven. That is why Jesus' admonition "to store up treasure in heaven" is so forward thinking. While there is little doubt that we want to make good use of our stay on this planet, the goal of our stewardship here is for eternal benefit and fruit in heaven.

I will be held accountable.

In II Corinthians 5:10, Paul warns the Corinthian church, "For we must all appear before the judgment seat of Christ, so that each one may be recompensed for his deeds in the body, according to what he has done, whether good or bad." This issue of the Christian being held accountable for deeds in the body is rarely addressed in the local church.

The picture is clear, however. The Christian will stand before the judgment seat of Christ and be held accountable for what he or she has done in their time on this earth. Similarly, in Matthew 25, the stewards, all of them, were called to account for their use of talents. The reality of accountability should sober the believer so that he or she will not be satisfied with "getting in the gates."

There is reward and loss.

In the same way that the believer will appear before the judgment seat of Christ, Paul also makes it clear that the believer will receive reward or loss at the judgment seat. I Corinthians 3:14-15 paints a vivid picture:

> If any man's work which he has built on it remains, he will receive a reward. If any man's work is burned up, he will suffer loss; but he himself will be saved, yet so as through fire.

I suspect that many of us are in for a frightful shock at the judgment seat of Christ. Much of what we did for our own sake or glory will be burnt up. The quiet servant and the faithful will receive reward. This prospect of judgment with resulting reward or loss should motivate the believe to be a wise steward and begin preparing now for "*that day.*" As Matthew Henry said, "The business of every day ought to be to prepare for *the* day."

Summary of Biblical Stewardship

The basics of biblical stewardship mentioned above are beginning points. We encourage each church to develop its own. Similarly, we encourage churches to expand on these points. Preach on these points. Conduct small groups like Crown Financial Ministry studies which teach on these points. Drive these points into your culture as the foundation of a culture of generosity.

What Is A Church Foundation?

The term foundation can be intimidating. It should not be. ***A church foundation is simply a tool by which a local church may receive cash gifts as well as noncash gifts.*** From a motivational sense, the church foundation provides a method to serve those members who want or need this option. There are three main types of church foundations and three methods for establishing them.

Types of Church Foundations

We often see three types of church foundations: an endowed church foundation, a capital fund, and an endowed missions fund.

An **endowed church foundation** is typically set up so that only the income from principal will be used. That income may be used to support some portion of church operations or new programs. We do not recommend that the church foundation be used to solely support the operations because such a foundation could take away all the incentive of members to give. At most, we would limit the amount of operational support to 50 percent, but this amount should be determined by each local church.

A **capital fund** is a designated fund which may receive cash and noncash gifts. Members may designate contributions to this fund to help with ongoing capital projects of the church. Typically, this fund is often a "pass through" fund, which means that while funds may accumulate in this capital fund, they will often be disbursed back out for some capital project. The capital fund "scratches the itch" of those wishing to give to something tangible.

An **endowed missions fund** is a designated fund which also may receive cash and noncash gifts. The purpose of this fund is to provide support for mission projects of the church. These projects may be projects of the church or for missions outside of the local church. This fund is often set up so that income from principal will be used in such a way that ongoing missions work might be sustained. For instance, a member might want to offer an ongoing "matching grant" for students wanting to go on mission trips—for every dollar a student raises, the fund "matches" with a corresponding dollar.

Methods of Establishing Church Foundations

There are three methods of establishing church foundations: one, denominational, two, "do it yourself" method, and three, Christian community foundations.

The **denominational** method assumes the denomination has a denominational foundation and is set up to help local churches set up their own foundation. A key question about this approach is whether the denomination is focused upon receiving gifts for the denomination or for the local church. Some denominations require that a certain percentage of the gift go to the denomination itself. You'll need to contact your denomination about its ability to serve your specific church.

The **"Do it Yourself Method"** typically means that a local church body sets up its own trust or does its own filing with the IRS to set up its foundation. This approach calls for the local church to run another entity, perform its own administration and provide its own expertise in receiving cash and noncash gifts. Additionally, under this approach, the local church assumes the resulting liability for any gifts, particularly noncash gifts, into this structure.

The **Christian community foundation** method means that the local church sets up what is called a "donor advised fund" with a Christian community foundation. There are many Christian community foundations around the country. Look at the website of the National Christian Foundation—www.nationalchristian.com for a listing. Each of the three types of funds—church foundation, capital fund and missions fund—may be set up. Under this approach, the Christian community foundation is considered the owner of the assets, and the local church provides a board of advisors who recommend grant distributions. The advantage of this approach is that the local church does not have to administer the foundation, and gains the expertise and ability to receive cash and noncash gifts. Similarly, the church does not show these assets on the books of the church financial statement.

How A Church Foundation Works

A church foundation has two basic goals: one, to serve members with gifting options, and two, to distribute funds. In recognizing these goals, there are three basic elements to understanding how a church foundation works:

1. Establishment of a church foundation
2. Promotion of the church foundation
3. Administration of the church foundation

Establishment of the Church Foundation

A church foundation is established by choosing one of the three methods above. Once you choose the method, then you take the appropriate steps to actually open the church foundation. The donor advised fund model is the quickest way to get started.

Under any model, you'll want to have a board of directors or advisors. If you choose to go the "do it yourself" method, you'll also need investment policy, conflict of interest, document retention/destruction policies etc. Under any model, you'll want to make an initial contribution to the foundation so that it is not "empty" of funds. An initial contribution gives some sense of accomplishment for those considering making contributions.

Promotion of the Church Foundation

Promotion of the church foundation will be discussed in more detail at **The Pathway to Growth.** Suffice it to say that a key function of the church foundation is to build awareness among members about its availability and utility. Without promotion, the foundation will not grow, and the church body will remain underserved.

Administration of the Church Foundation

Once the foundation is established and promotion begins, the next question is "what does the church do when it begins to receive gift inquiries." Generally, those questions should come in to one person at the church—either an executive pastor, stewardship pastor or stewardship committee chair. If the gift can be handled by the church, usually cash or publicly traded stock, then the church should handle the gift. But if the gift has more complexity, then the gift may be referred to an outside expert, a board member or if a donor advised fund is used, to the staff of the Christian community foundation for handling.

Recognize that a church should be prepared to receive cash, publicly traded stock and all forms of noncash gifts as well. Accordingly, the church should have a gift acceptance policy and the appropriate people to handle such gifts or rely upon outside advisors to make those gifts happen.

Why Is A Church Foundation Important?

A church foundation is important for many reasons. At the heart, while a church may preach about God's ownership we know that churches are at the bottom percentage of organizations receiving estate and planned gifts. We also know that individuals are often reluctant to make significant gifts to churches because of leadership turnover and uncertainty over whether the funds would be used wisely. Clearly, these individuals are reluctant to leave such large gifts to the general fund.

A church foundation provides the means and the credibility to receive such funds. It is a designated form of giving. Additionally, a church foundation connotes larger gifts, including estate gifts.

From a statistical perspective, we know that 80 percent of all giving in the United States comes in the form of cash gifts. On the other hand, the wealth of the world is in noncash assets—90 percent. Stated differently, the church today is receiving gifts from the smallest piece of the pie. As such, it has a significant opportunity to help people begin receiving noncash gifts.

The Pathway to Growth

The pathway to growth for a church foundation involves three steps: awareness, education and options, and advocacy.

Awareness

1. Leadership Awareness.

The first level of awareness begins with the pastor, then staff and board. We often encourage the leadership to make sure that they have their own planning completed. This allows them to share a testimony of how the foundation has benefited them.

2. Church Foundation Brochure

We encourage the publication of a church foundation brochure. The brochure should list the mission and vision of the church and the purpose of the foundation. It should additionally list the services and types of gifts the foundation can receive. The brochure should be made available in public places in the church and announced from the pulpit. We also encourage bulletin announcements and newsletter announcements.

3. Special Groups

Awareness should also be produced within specialized audiences within the churches. Professional advisors (attorneys, accountants, brokers, life insurance professionals, etc.) should be invited to a special awareness reception. Seniors should be made aware as well as business owners.

Education and Options

In addition to a church foundation brochure, the church should also seek to provide ongoing education about giving options, including gifts of vehicles, real estate, business interests, collectibles, business inventory, charitable gift annuities, and wills and trusts. The checklist looks like a funnel.

Note that with each option, brochures and informational pieces should be created.

Advocacy

Growth of the church foundation can be enchanced by the testimonies of people who have used the foundation. These testimonies will serve as advocates for the foundation and encourage others to use the foundation.

These advocates can be produced through **Forums of 12**. In essence, Forums of 12 is an invitation only event where the pastor and other leadership invite individuals who may have planning needs. At the Forum, they are taught basics of biblical stewardship and provided with some planning tips. The Forum is designed to take only one and a half hours and can take place at lunch, dinner or a dessert.

Next Steps: Preparing Your Plan

Now that we've provided you with this brief summary of your church foundation, you are probably ready to get started. Don't be overwhelmed by the process. Take some small steps now and begin moving forward. We see more church foundations stalled by "analysis paralysis."

If your church has not established a foundation, gather the necessary people and seek to get it approved. Remember that the best time to launch the foundation is early in the year so you can build awareness and then by year-end you may be ready to receive some year-end noncash gifts.

If your church has established a foundation, then work on your awareness and promotion plan. We suggest that you set forth three to five promotional activities and materials for the course of the year. Keep in mind that one of your highest return activities is the Forums of 12. Just take that next step!

~~~

William F. High is the President/General Counsel of the Servant Christian Community Foundation (www.servantchristian.com). He may be reached at whigh@servantchristian.com. Servant's mission is to inspire, teach and facilitate revolutionary biblical generosity. Servant works with givers, ministries and financial advisors to help increase giving using cash and noncash assets.
~~~

Glossary

424A

A standard application form used by various federal grant programs; designed to adapt nonprofit applications for multiple grant programs

424B

A standard application form used by various federal grant programs; contains the various assurances required of a nonprofit

501(c)3

A charitable organization that is organized and operated solely for tax-exempt purposes; cannot benefit private shareholders or engage in lobbying

509(1)a

A government-recognized type of charity; primarily includes churches, schools, hospitals, and other organizations that receive most of their public support from gifts, grants, and contributions from a variety of people

509(1)b

Charities that receive their support from gifts, grants, contributions and fees for their tax-exempt services

A

Anecdotal data

Data comprised of professional opinions, expert viewpoints, or statements made by those influenced by the nonprofit; essentially, any data that is not statistical

Allowable costs

Costs the donor agrees to reimburse per the contract with the nonprofit

Budget justification

A clarification of the budget that explains how dollar amounts were determined; this is not an explanation for the amounts requested

B

Budget narrative

Explains the budget; can include the source of costs, the itemization of totals, the purpose of purchased supplies and services, and the justification for the size of salaries, fringe benefits, and indirect costs

Builder generation

Also known as traditionalists; the generation that fought during World War II

C

Capacity building

Activities that strengthen the skills, abilities, processes, and resources that organizations need to function; includes training, human resource development, and organizational development

Capital funds

Funds used to obtain fixed assets such as land, buildings, building additions, and equipment

Catalog of Federal Domestic Assistance (CFDA)

A database provided by the U.S. Government that lists all domestic assistance programs funded by the government; for use by individuals, local and state governments, and organizations; available in print and online (www.cfda.gov)

Cause-related marketing

A type of marketing that involves the effort of a for-profit business and a nonprofit organization for mutual benefit; a percentage of the businesses' sales revenue is donated to the nonprofit

Charitable gift annuity

A nonprofit regularly pays a fixed sum of money during the lifetime(s) of one or two people in exchange for an irrevocable transfer of cash or property

Charitable lead trust

A nonprofit receives income from an asset during a set time period or during the donor's lifetime. Once that contract expires, the asset reverts to the donor's estate

Charitable remainder trust

A donor receives income for a set time period or for his/her lifetime from an asset donated to a nonprofit. Once the contract expires, the asset reverts to the nonprofit

Charitable Solicitation Registration (CSR) laws

Many states require organizations to register with the state before soliciting contributions; depending on the state, some organizations are exempt from registration if they meet certain criteria

Charitable trust

A trust that promotes education, public health, poverty relief, religion, or any charitable purpose as defined by law; can have perpetual existence; is completely or partially exempt from taxes

Community foundation

An organization supported by donations from local residents; distributes endowment funds for charitable purposes

Corporate foundation

A charitable foundation that distributes a corporation's profits to nonprofit organizations

D

Demonstration grant

Funds used to study the feasibility of a new project or program

Direct costs

Expenses directly attributed to the completion of a grant project; includes salaries, fringe benefits, travel, equipment, supplies, professional development, consulting services, etc.

Donor-advised fund

A fund in a community foundation or a public charity where the donor or a committee selected by the donor recommends charities to support; the foundation or public charity can accept or reject these recommendations

E

Endowment

When some gifts are donated to a nonprofit, the donor stipulates that the principal amount must remain intact. This principal is invested to create a source of income for the charity. Donors may require that this principal amount remain intact for perpetuity or for a certain length of time

Equivalency determination

The assessment of whether a non-U.S. charity is the equivalent of a U.S. public charity

F

Form 990

An information return form that most public charities must submit to the IRS annually

G

Gift Planning

Helping people define and achieve their charitable giving objectives in an efficient and effective way while balancing their personal, financial and family realities.

Grants.gov

The online source for finding and applying for federal grants (www.grants.gov)

H

Hard data

Statistical information

I

Income-producing ministry

A nonprofit's idea or product that is sold to produce income

Indirect costs

Costs that are not directly related to the cost object; includes items like taxes, administration, and personnel

In-kind resources

Resources that have cash value, but do not consist of cash; includes items like office supplies, computers, building material, technology assistance, etc.

L

Limited Liability Company (LLC)

A business company that combines the limited liability of a corporation with the pass-through income taxation of a partnership

M

Matching funds

Funds that will be supplied to a nonprofit to "match" the exact dollar amount raised from the nonprofit's other sources

Memoranda of Understanding

A document describing an agreement between parties that indicates a common action plan; often used in situations that do not suggest a legal commitment

N

Need statement

A description of the nonprofit's proposed project; presents evidence for the need of the nonprofit's project or program; proves the nonprofit is capable of addressing the need

O

OMB Circular A-122—Cost Principles for Nonprofit Organizations

A statement of government policy that establishes methods for determining the costs of grants, contracts, and other agreements with non-profit organizations

Operating support

Donations that cover a nonprofit's daily expenses such as salaries, utility bills, or office supplies

Organizational governance

The policies, structures, and processes a nonprofit uses to control its activities and achieve its goals

P

Private foundation

A nonprofit organization typically established by one individual or family; subject to excise taxes and to more restrictions that are not applicable to public charities

Private operating foundation

A nonprofit organization, typically established by one individual or family, that conducts its own programs and directly donates funds for charitable purposes

Public charity

A nonprofit organization exempt from federal income tax under Section 501(c)3 of the IRS tax code that usually receives most of its support from the general public; some organizations exempt under Section 501(c)3 must meet a public support test before being considered a public charity

R

Request for Proposal (RFP)

A written notification stating that a grant-making organization is seeking qualified nonprofits to support; contains a list of the project details and the application process

Revocable living trust

A written document that gives a trustee the responsibility of managing the donor's property for the benefit of those who will receive the property after the donor's death; this trust is revocable because the donor is able to change or end the trust at any point (provided he/she is still mentally competent)

S

Standard Form 269

A form used to prepare financial reports for a grant

U

Unallowable costs

Costs not allowed per the terms and conditions of the grant award

V

Venture philanthropy

A combination of long-term investment procedures and venture capital processes where a financial investment is made to a nonprofit in order to build capacity and to produce results

Notes

[1] "Quick Facts about Nonprofits." *National Center for Charitable Statistics.* Urban Institute. 2009. Web. 30 November 2009.

[2] *Foundation Directory Online*. Foundation Center, 2009. Web. 30 November 2009.

[3] Blackwood, Amy, Kennard T. Wing, and Thomas H. Pollak. "The Nonprofit Sector in Brief, Facts & Figures from the *Nonprofit Almanac 2008*: Public Charities, Giving, and Volunteering." *National Center for Charitable Statistics*. 2008. Web. 5 September 2009.

[4] Luke 17:11-17. *New American Standard Bible*. Kenneth Baker, gen. Ed. Grand Rapids: Zondervan, 1995.

[5] I.R.C. § 4945(d)(4) (2005); Reg. § 53.4945-5(a).

[6] Bruce R. Hopkins. The Law of Tax-Exempt Organizations. 9th ed. Washington: Lerner Law Book, 2007. 55.

[7] Rev. Proc. 92-94, 1992-1 C.B. 507, Reg. § 53.4945-6(c)-(2)(ii), § 53.4942(a)-3(a)(6), and § 53.4945-5(a)(5).

[8] This can be done through reasonable reliance upon a written legal opinion of the equivalence, through analysis of facts contained in an affidavit by the foreign charity leading the foundation to find equivalence, or through reliance on recognition of the foreign entity by the IRS as a 501(c)(3) public charity.

[9] *See e.g.*, the 2005 version of its Voluntary Best Practices for U.S.-Based Charities *available at* http://www.treas.gov/offices/enforcement/key-issues/protecting/docs/guidelines_charities.pdf.

[10] Internal Revenue Service. "Governance and Related Topics." *IRS*, 4 Feb. 2008. Web. 2009.

[11] Internal Revenue Service. "Good Governance Practices For 501(c)(3) Organizations." *IRS*, 7 Feb. 2007. Web. 2009.

[12] As used on Form 990 "independent" generally refers to directors that are not financially significantly benefited by the organization (nor are their family members or business interests).

[13] Eric Kelderman. "IRS Discloses 2009 Plans for Reviewing Tax-Exempt Organizations." *The Chronicle of Philanthropy* 25 November 2008. Print.

[14] *Bubbling Well Church of Universal Love, Inc. v. Comm'r*, 74 T.C. 531 (1980), ("The domination of an organization's board by one family does not necessarily disqualify it for exemption, however it does provide an obvious opportunity for abuse of tax-exemption, and therefore there must be open and candid disclosure of

all facts of the organization, including its finances and operations.")

[15] New Hampshire, *e.g.*

[16] Regs. 1.501(c)(3)-1(c)(2)

[17] Bader, Barry S. and Elaine Zablocki. "Executive Compensation: Prepare to Defend Your Process and Executive Pay." *Great Boards*, Spring 2009. Web. 2009.

[18] This recommendation, found in the 2005 version of its Voluntary Best Practices for U.S.-Based Charities, is based upon the June 2005 final report to Congress of the Panel on the Nonprofit Sector.

[19] Browning, Beverly, A. "Winning Strategies for Developing Grant Proposals." 2nd ed. Washington: Government Information Services, 2005. 20. ("For organizations that spend a total of $500,000 or more in federal funds (calculated based on awards from all federal programs) – an audit by a private, independent outside legal or accounting firm is required.")

[20] The support test requires that 1/3 of our total support comes from the public. In figuring this 1/3, the most noteworthy part of this test is the 2% rule. This rule takes 2% of the total support and says that is the amount that any one donor (including private individuals as well as corporations and other organizations) can give to be counted as public support. Anything in excess of that 2% figure is considered "non-public" support.

[21] Hopkins, Bruce. R. "The Law of Fundraising." 4th ed. Hoboken: Wiley, John & Sons, 2009.

[22] Hopkins, Bruce. R. "The Law of Fundraising." 4th ed. Hoboken: Wiley, John & Sons, 2009. ("About a dozen states exclude from the term *solicitation* the process of applying for a government grant. Occasionally state law provides that the word *contribution* includes a grant from a government agency or excludes the quest for a grant from a private foundation.").

[23] For a discussion of recent actions taken against charities and fines imposed, see Jamie Usry's 2008 web article *Charitable Solicitation Within the Nonprofit Sector: Paving the Regulatory Landscape for Future Success.*

[24] Leech, Beth L. "Funding Faction or Buying Silence? Grants, Contracts, and Interest Group Lobbying Behavior." *Policies Study Journal* 34.1 (1 Feb. 2006). n. pag. Web. 2009.

[25] *County Allegheny v. American Civil Liberties Union*, 492 U.S. 573, 591 (1989).

[26] *Laskowski v. Spellings*, 443 F.3d 930 (7th Cir. 2006); *Americans United for Separation v. Prison Fellow.*, 509 F.3d 406 (8th Cir. 2007).

[27] "Organizations Seeking Grants." *Ford Foundation.* The Ford Foundation, 2009. Web. 5 Oct. 2009.

[28] *Catalogue of Federal Domestic Assistance*. General Services Administration. n.d. Web. 25 Sept. 2009.

[29] "Rural Health Care Services Outreach Program." HRSA Electronic Handbook for Applicants/Grantee. U.S. Department of Health and Human Services, n.d. Web. 28 Sept. 2009.

[30] "Rural Health Care Services Outreach Program." HRSA Electronic Handbook for Applicants/Grantee. U.S. Department of Health and Human Services, n.d. Web. 28 Sept. 2009.

[31] "New American Standard Bible (NASB)." Kenneth Baker, gen. Ed. Grand Rapids: Zondervan, 1995.

CPSIA information can be obtained at www.ICGtesting.com
Printed in the USA
LVOW131940160512

281986LV00001B/4/P

9 781609 572983